Admissions
Confidential

Admissions Confidential

An Insider's
Account of the
Elite College
Selection
Process

Rachel Toor

St. Martin's Griffin
New York

www.stmartins.com

Library of Congress Cataloging-in-Publication Data

Toor, Rachel.
    Admissions confidential : an insider's account of the elite
college selection process / Rachel Toor.
        p. cm.
    ISBN 0-312-28405-5 (hc)
    ISBN 0-312-30235-5 (pbk)
        1. Universities and colleges—United States—Admission.
2. Duke University—Admission. 3. College administrators—
United States—Biography. I. Title.

LB2351.2 T66 2001
378.1'61—dc21   2001034892

D10 9 8

For my cute little mother,

Marcelle Lapow Toor

Contents

Note to Reader

This is a true story, based on my experiences during the three years I worked in the admissions office at Duke University. My descriptions of the application process, and my opinions, observations, and concerns about the process, are real and genuine. However, the names of student applicants, of their schools, and of other persons and places associated with the application process have been changed or withheld. The identities of applicants and the content of their applications have also been disguised and in many instances are fictional composites or prototypes. In chapter 5 actual student essays have been reproduced with the permission of the applicants.

Preface

"We're not rejecting them, we're just denying them admission."

I never wanted to write about college admissions. I don't find it particularly interesting, nor do I consider myself a great big expert on the topic. I was at first surprised, and later alarmed, to learn of the intense fascination many people apparently have with the process of being admitted to highly selective American colleges and universities.

After three years of working in Duke's Office of Undergraduate Admissions, however, I realized that I am troubled by this business. I am troubled by the ways parents invest and insinuate themselves into their children's applications; troubled by the stress and anxiety endured by American high school students who feel that they must busy themselves for four years in order to get into a "good" college; I am troubled by the inequities and class bias, the ways you can buy access, both to information and, ultimately, to admission; finally I am troubled by the arbitrariness of the decision-making process and by the qualifications and intellectual merits of those who are sitting in judgment of the applicants.

Ultimately I find myself coming back, again and again, to the same question: Does it matter where you go to college? Many people think it does.

It would have been easy to make a buck after leaving my job in admissions. I could have set up my own independent college counseling business and charged lots of money for my "insider knowledge." Or I could have written a how-to book, giving away the "secrets" of how you, as an applicant, can improve the odds that you will receive an A for admission.

Palliative pabulum. There are no real secrets, just a process. It's a process that is at its most profound level simply human, all too human. When I pondered what I thought would be helpful for kids and their families, I realized that what I would want to know is the day-to-dayness of it all, the way things actually work. Who does the job and how do they do it?

This book is about one person's experience at one place. Readers will no doubt realize that some of Duke's practices are peculiar to Duke; many of them, however, are not unlike those at similarly highly selective private colleges and universities. I was not, I suspect, a typical admissions officer. But, if during the time I was working at Duke you applied from my region of responsibility, I was what you got. Ethnology is the discipline of looking closely at a specific culture, trying to get a sense of what you can learn not only about that narrow strip of interest but also what that might ultimately tell us about ourselves. I like to think of myself as a cub anthropologist, like a cub reporter or a Cub Scout. By giving my view of one specific place, I hope to allow readers a peek inside an arcane process so that they can arm themselves with questions— rather than answers—when they enter this strange world of college admissions.

The book follows the seasons of the admissions cycle. It begins in the summer with the hiring and training of new admissions officers. Fall is spent recruiting, traveling to the regions of the country that send the largest numbers of applicants (even if you read applications from North Dakota, you're not likely to score a trip to Fargo). Early decision begins in November and is finished well before the holidays. After the first of the year reading season begins, an intense period that lasts until the last week of February; selection committee rounds are generally in the first week of March. Decisions are mailed in early April; May is filled with more recruiting, both of admitted applicants and of the new crop of juniors who will enter the following year. And then it's summer again. Though I spent a total of three years working in admissions at Duke, I've chosen to tell the story of my first year, to allow the reader to understand, as I came to, the surprising, sometimes shocking, truths about the way the system works. This book is meant to be an evocative, rather than exhaustive, description of the process.

Duke's office is, I think, no better or worse than its peers. It is, simply, the one I experienced. There are bright people working in admissions, and some folks who are stunningly less capable—as you'd find in any industry. And like other professions, admissions has its own language and conventions, its own rhythms, and its own internal logic.

After reading this book I hope kids and their parents will go into the college application process realizing that it's not necessarily fair, it's not necessarily meritocratic, and even if they do everything "right," they still can't be assured that they will get what they think they want. I hope that, understanding this, families will refocus their efforts, away from attaining the Holy Grail of admission to a particular elite school and toward the realization that there are many great colleges and universities in this country, many places where students will be happy and can acquire a good education. And that if they don't get into their dream school, it is only their application that is being denied.

I loved being an admissions officer. I believed that Duke was overall a good place and more, I loved the kids who applied, loved becoming a part of their lives. It was a rare week when I didn't have at least a couple of "my" kids—those Duke students whose applications I'd read—drop by the office to say hello during the school year. But as much as I enjoyed the job—thought it was fun, thought it was easy—there were also parts of it that I found troubling. While acting as an admissions officer, I tended to skim over those things, brushing them aside in the interests of getting the work done. It is only after having left the profession that it has become easier to talk about the inequities and the flawed humanity of the process of admission to highly selective schools.

In this book I use the "historical present" tense when I talk about my time in admissions. When I say "we," I mean "we" in the sense that I was representing Duke and was told, by and large, what to say and do. What I said and did, however, was my own interpretation of the instructions I received. Each of my colleagues could write their own book about their time in and take on the profession; each would no doubt be vastly different from mine. I hope the reader will use this book not as a weapon against admissions professionals ("Is it true what she says about . . . ?") but as a tool to ask informed questions about the process.

A few years before I started working in admissions, I wrote an essay for a national weekly publication, *The Chronicle of Higher Education*. It was about the relationship between authors and editors of academic books. It was my "Dear John" letter to the world of scholarly publishing. In the fall of what I knew would be my last year working in admissions, I got an out-of-the-blue E-mail from an editor at *The Chronicle*, asking if I would be willing to write another piece for them.

One thing led to another and I got a gig doing a regular column. (They wanted me to write on admissions, but I said I wouldn't while I was still working for Duke.) I also started doing radio commentaries for WUNC, my local NPR affiliate in North Carolina. Those personal statements (or parts of them), essays about living life connected to a university, lead off most of the chapters in this book.

The rest of the book is my "Dear John" letter to college admissions.

Introduction

Farewell to an Idea

"We're juniors."

She's smiling at me with teeth as pearly as the single-strand around her cashmere-encased neck. She has yellow-white hair that can only be called "coiffed." Standing behind her and a little to the side is a sullen creature with stringy hair, a nose ring, cargo jeans and a tanned puppy-fattish belly that peeks out beneath a tight Abercrombie T-shirt.

"Excuse me?" Though befuddled, I'm trying to be polite.

"We're juniors," says the glamorous fifty-something, "and we're thinking about applying to Duke. What can you tell us about your premed program? How many of your students are accepted to Harvard for medical school? What is the major most likely to gain a student acceptance? And tell me, please, do you have a chapter of Kappa Kappa?"

I'm standing in the gym of Dwight Academy, a long-time preparer of young men—and now young women—for the Ivy League and other highly selective colleges and universities. It smells weirdly of teenaged sweat and Chanel No. 5.

As an admissions officer at Duke University I travel around the country whipping kids (and their parents) into a frenzy so that they will apply. I tell them how great a school Duke is academically and how much fun they will have socially. Then, come April, we reject most of them. We don't call it rejecting, though. We're "denying" them admission.

Most of the students I meet on my travels are BWRKs. That's admissionsese for bright well-rounded kids. You know, the ones who do everything right. They take honors classes, study hard enough to be in the top 10 percent of their class, get solid 1350s on their SATs, play sports, participate in student government, do community service (sometimes even when it's not required). They're earnest, they're hardworking, they're determined. They do everything right, and most of them don't have a chance of getting in. We deny them. In droves. Another BWRK. Zip. How boring.

It's the nature of highly selective college and university admissions at this point in time that the applicant pool is bigger and stronger than it's ever been. We reckon that of the kids who apply, 80 percent of them, if admitted, could succeed academically. But the numbers work in our favor, and we admit more like 20 percent of our applicants (except for early decision, in which the admit rate is 40 percent). So we end up denying applicants who look perfectly good to us, and exceptional to their parents, their schools, and their peers. Being bright and well rounded just isn't enough. Many schools now are looking for what they call "angular" kids, those with a much more focused interest or talent, kids who have done all the typical stuff and then have pursued an interest or a passion to an nth degree—doing publishable research, playing with a major philharmonic, acting in films. With so many applicants looking so much alike, they need to find a way to make themselves stand out.

I made my own college choice in a random and haphazard way: I'd spent the summer after eleventh grade in France, working on the restoration of a twelfth-century château in the Loire Valley. It sounds better and more impressive than it was: basically I just hauled around loads of dusty rocks. I lived in an ancient schoolhouse with a group of American high school and college students, and a few French ones as well. Most of the high school kids there were focused, to the point of obsession, on their college applications. Coming from a mediocre public school in upstate New York, I was horrified to find that, having not given it much thought, I was going to be left behind. Panic set in. I listened but did not contribute to endless "where do you want to go, where do you think you'll get in, what is your safety school" conversations. I didn't know, at that point, what a safety school was.

I desperately wanted to go to Yale, a school I had never visited and knew almost nothing about, because of two men I met that summer. They were among the most brilliant, arrogant, knowledgeable, and obnoxious people I'd ever encountered. They terrified me. I wanted to be just like them. I sent away for the application.

I didn't apply early decision because I didn't know about early decision.

I got lucky, and was admitted to Yale. I first saw the place when

I matriculated. It was a rainy, awful day. My mother and I made the trip and got hopelessly lost on the many one-way streets. The city was grimy and the campus far from the idyllic pastoral I had imagined. I made this choice because of two arrogant geeks. And now it was too late.

My college choice shaped me in ways that I can't even begin to measure. While I was there I never used the words "Yale" and "happy" in the same sentence. I learned to talk about books I hadn't read, a skill that took me years to unlearn. I woke up to class consciousness, to differences in sexuality, in race, religion, and ethnicity—issues that had never come up in my provincial high school. I was awed by classmates who had gone to boarding school and seemed so much worldlier—because they were—than I.

My senior year at Yale I took a course—one of the residential college seminars taught by professionals from the "real world"—on editing for argument. The teacher, at the time an editor at Oxford University Press, convinced me that I should try publishing.

I fell into my job in admissions just as I fell into my career in scholarly publishing. After college I began working at Oxford University Press and stayed until I was promoted as high up the ladder as I cared to go. Then I decided to leave publishing, leave New York, and leave my marriage. On my way out the door to a new adventure, hoping to end up as a ranch hand in Wyoming, I was recruited to be an acquisitions editor at Duke University Press, a small southern upstart. I knew very little about the press, or about the South for that matter. I had never even been on the far side of the Mason-Dixon line. But I had read a lot of Faulkner. I'd seen

Deliverance. I worried that everyone would drive around in pickups, chewing tobacco and spitting. I thought southern culture was a contradiction in terms. I moved to Durham, North Carolina.

After five years at Duke Press I was again ready for change and decided to apply to medical school. First I had to go back and take all of the premed hard-science courses I'd managed to avoid at Yale. I applied, got in, and then decided not to go. I took a year off and spent it freelance editing, doing some of my own writing, but mostly riding horses and running. I spent that summer in California hanging out and decided, though I wasn't quite ready to move to the left coast, I did want to find a way to get back out there.

I started talking to people I knew at Duke, looking for a job that would be fun, and to be honest, not as intellectually demanding as being an editor. I'd burned out on helping academics write better books. It's hard work: First you have to figure out which books are worth publishing, which monographs on seemingly narrow topics might make big contributions to a field. Then you have to really look at the manuscript, seeing both what is there and what is not there, understanding where the author wants to go with her argument and then helping her get there. Ultimately, it's invisible work—only you and the author know what your contribution to the project has been. When the book gets published, it's the author's book. You bask in reflected glory, if you bask at all.

I was ready to be less invisible. So I began calling everyone I knew—and even some people I didn't—trying to find a job at Duke. I wanted to be at Duke because I liked living in Durham. And I wanted to continue to work in a university setting.

Through my running club I was acquainted with a woman who

had been at Duke almost her whole life. She'd gone to the school as an undergraduate and had never left; she'd worked her way to an upper-level post in administration. I asked if she'd be willing to talk with me about potential jobs, and she said she'd be delighted.

While we spoke she shuffled through stacks of paper, doing some kind of sorting work, the nature of which was not apparent to me. She asked what kinds of things I might be interested in. I really didn't know, I told her, but I did want to have less responsibility and more of a public presence.

"Admissions," she said.

She explained a little about the job, that it's partly going out on the road and recruiting, partly staying at home and reading applications. That seemed similar to what I'd done as an editor, but also a lot easier: a handful of pages written by seventeen year olds versus five-hundred-page manuscripts written by old people with Ph.D.'s. Sounded pretty good to me. She gave me the name of the director of undergraduate admissions and told me to use her name when I contacted him.

I wrote him a long letter, introducing myself and giving some background about the twelve years I'd spent in scholarly publishing. Ultimately I asked if he would be available to chat with me, regardless of whether they were looking to fill positions, so that I could gain a better understanding of what the process was about.

I was surprised to receive, some weeks later, from Duke's Office of Undergraduate Admissions, a form letter telling me that there were no positions currently available and thanking me for my application.

Finally, with a little persistence and a lot of help from friends and acquaintances, I ended up in the office of the director. He was surprisingly easy. Apparently my letter had never made it to him: it had been tossed into the trash by the committee of senior admissions staff members charged with screening job applicants. I had been deemed "overqualified." I've since realized that the process of how you get hired gives you a certain amount of insight into how it will be to work at a place.

The director was warm and personable and forthcoming. In the last month or so they had just hired five new admissions officers but had the latitude to take on more. By the time I left his office, it seemed clear to me that I was going to be offered a job. There remained, however, a few hoops to jump. I had to go through the formal interview process, which turned out to be surprisingly elaborate: a half day of interviews, first with the admissions officers, those people who would be my peers, and then with the "associates," the associate directors who formed the next layer of the hierarchy. And then there was the presentation. Each prospective admissions officer is asked to give a fifteen-minute oral presentation to the entire staff on a subject of his or her choice.

My first set of interviews was with three young women, all admissions officers, two of whom were leaving. All three had gone to Duke. One, quick and savvy, was off to graduate school in English. We had an interesting and lively conversation about the Duke English department. At one time, in the mid- to late eighties, it had been the hottest in the country. We talked about the literary critic Stanley Fish. The women interviewing me know him only as the intimidating Professor Fish; they marvel at my calling him

Stanley, that I know him as my former boss at Duke Press and consider him a friend.

The other interviewer, a funny and friendly African American woman, had just accepted a job at a lesser school doing minority recruiting. She was smart and enthusiastic and I asked if she had done minority recruiting at Duke. No, she answered brusquely. They hint, both of the women who are leaving, at difficulties they had working with the director.

The third woman, Missy, is staying. She tells me that she wanted to be an admissions officer ever since taking her own college tour. She had traveled the country with her mother the summer before her senior year in high school, visiting colleges. After this grand tour she was still uncertain where she wanted to go, but she knew one thing for sure: she wanted a career in admissions. We started talking in general about the Duke student body, about the zeitgeist of the place. I said I'd heard my friends on the Duke faculty complain that their students never challenged them, that the kids tended to imbibe information dully and without questioning.

"How can you question these professors?" Missy pleaded. "They wrote the textbook!"

Next I met with two of the "associates." The man was leaving, going to be a college counselor at a private high school. "The other side of the desk" is what they call it. This is a fairly standard career path, it turns out. The woman had bucked the trend and had come to admissions from that very side of the desk—she had worked previously at a private school and had come to Durham with her husband. He and one of her two sons had attended Duke, and she, as if by proxy, had a great love for the school even though she was not an alumna.

The woman and I had a fine talk, earnest and serious. The man who was leaving said little, save for a sarcastic comment every now and then. He seemed glad to be leaving.

In the afternoon I was to do my presentation. I decided that I would prepare two different talks, each based on book projects. As I was leaving my editorial job at Duke Press I'd been given a contract to write a book of my own, a history of the Duke University Primate Center, founded some thirty years ago by my friend Peter Klopfer, a zoologist, and his colleague in anthropology, John Buettner-Janusch.

I decided for my talk that I would skip the history of the center's founding and focus on the career of the famous and flamboyant Buettner-Janusch after he'd left Duke. He had gone on to New York University, where he'd been caught using his university laboratory to manufacture illegal drugs. He went to trial acting as his own lawyer and was thrown into jail. Upon his release he mailed chocolates laced with poison to several of his old enemies, including the federal judge who had sentenced him. The next time he was put away for much longer, and ended up dying in prison.

The other topic was another book project I was currently working on. Also just before leaving Duke Press I discovered that a colleague there, a designer, was as fanatical as I about Peeps. Not Pepys, the diarist. Not peep shows. But Peeps, the little yellow marshmallow chicks that show up around Easter time each year. We came at our love for them from different vantage points. As a child, my coauthor loved the shape of Peeps. She claims it was the beauty, the simplicity of their form, that led her to become a designer. I was a little Jewish girl who, growing up, was forbidden to eat candy. It wasn't until I got to college that I discovered the ambrosial deliciousness of Peeps (particularly when they were stale).

So we decided to do a book. *Peeps: Food or Fetish* was going to be a beautifully designed coffee table book. We weren't the only ones, it turns out, obsessed by Peeps. There's a whole Peep culture out there. The Internet is rich with Peepness. We would collect art made with Peeps, haikus and other writings about them, and have a whole section called Recipeeps. My coauthor's house became the test kitchen. We had friends and family bring Peeps with them on their travels; we had photographs of Peeps at the Pyramids, Peeps drinking Ouzo on the Aegean, Peeps in front of Big Ben. We had literary agents in New York representing us.

When it came time for my presentation I stood up and told them that I wanted some insight into the office, and so I thought I'd experience firsthand how they make decisions. I had two topics on which I was prepared to speak. They could decide which one they heard.

The director polled the group. While there were factions on both sides, the majority seemed to want to go for the serious rather than the wacky. So I gave my little talk about the Primate Center.

After I finished there were a few polite questions. Then the director said, "Okay, now let's hear the Peeps."

So I ended up giving both talks. The Peeps were the clear favorite. For weeks after I'd been hired, people would come up to me and ask about the Peeps. Unfortunately, having a full-time job is not compatible with doing a lot of writing. I shelved the Primate Center book. Our agents sent out the Peeps proposal to a number of big publishers (they sent them out with packages of Peeps). We got a handful of lovely rejections. Most said the same thing, It's a great idea, but who wants to buy a full-color coffee table book on Peeps? If we scaled back the design and made it more text-heavy, they'd be interested. They returned the proposal, but no one sent back the Peeps. My coauthor didn't want to downgrade the design, so we gave up.

I was hired as an admissions officer.

1

Space May Create New Worlds: *Settling In*

One of the least attractive features of life in the Academy is the emphasis on credentials and the constant comparisons that go on: between the degreed and the nondegreed, between the elitely educated and the products of lesser institutions, between those who teach and those who publish. It's easy to measure productivity by the number of ball bearings produced or the number of burgers flipped; when it comes to evaluating qualities of mind, it's a murkier business.

"Smart" becomes a kind of essential signifier. "It's a smart book" means it's a book that will win the biggest prize in the field. "A smart critique" means someone has savaged someone. "He's really smart," whispered in hushed reverence, tells you he's up for a Nobel. You almost never hear the term "brilliant" in conversation, unless it's deployed in that favored phrase, "Brilliant but flawed." Like poor Mr. Ramsay in Virginia Woolf's *To the Lighthouse*, who sees thought as an alphabet, everyone is trying to figure out the letter they've landed on. Or gotten stuck on.

The university is naturally a hierarchical place, but the hierarchies can be confusing. Sometimes it seems that those at the top are not necessarily those whose minds are farthest along on the alphabet—how many administrators have written Really Important Books? A few, to be sure. But the job takes a different skill set. That's not to say that academic administration isn't challenging intellectual work. Budgeting and strategic planning and figuring out where to put a new art museum are nothing to sneeze at in terms of brainpower. How much easier it must be to do such tasks in the context of the Real World, rather than in a university, where being powerful is about having powerful ideas, where individuals (OK, only a few) can effect paradigm shifts in ways of looking at the world. The big dogs in Academe are the thinkers, not the managers.

But between administrators and scholars are a host of people who choose to live tied to academic life, but not as academics. Sometimes it's because of the people they love. Their spouses or partners are academics. Sometimes it's because the Real World seems less interesting or because most college towns are, let's face it, nice places to live. Or sometimes they came to a place when they were eighteen years old and never managed to leave.

Some of the smartest people I know have no Ph.D., because they either never finished graduate school or never started. ABD's (all but Dissertation) and NWD's (never wanted dissertation) are abundant in academic life. They are directors of university presses, public-relations gurus, teachers of freshman composition, editors of alumni magazines, vice presidents for student affairs, speechwriters, directors of development, and deans of undergraduate admissions. They are also people with terminal degrees—social workers and librarians. All are essential to running academic institutions—yet, unfortunately, they don't get much respect.

In the slash between faculty/staff lies a world of difference. Or as an ABD I know says, there are two categories in the university: faculty and not.

Not much money, prestige, or power comes with being an academic, but even less comes with not being an academic and hanging around an academic setting. I don't think I suffer from Ph.D. envy. I never wanted to go to graduate school. After falling into scholarly publishing right out of college, I didn't want to limit myself, to narrow my focus the way one must in order to get a doctorate. I liked being able to flit around different disciplines; I embraced my status as a dilettante.

As an acquisitions editor, I did enjoy a certain kind of organizational respect. At least to the authors I worked with, I was Oxford University Press and then Duke University Press. Switching to admissions, it's been a whole new thing. Any trace of respect for my organizational affiliation has dried up. Admissions folks are generally well-dressed, shiny, happy people, who don't tend to be regarded as intellectual heavyweights by the professoriate. My academic friends seemed to have some vague understanding that someone in the university was bringing in students; who those people were and how they did it were a bit of a mystery.

Many admissions officers don't really know how to deal with faculty members. Some treat professors with the same fawning admiration they had for them as students. It's hard enough for graduate students to make the transition from ephebe to colleague; it's even harder for those in, but not of, the academy. Other folks in admissions—often at the management level—work hard to keep faculty members at arm's length. "They don't understand how we do our jobs," the argument goes. "The more they know, the more trouble they'll make."

There are wonderful things about being in, but not of, the academy. It is darn nice to have an office on a campus. I like being able to take short walks in the middle of the day or to have coffee with a zoologist. Or a political scientist. Or a speechwriter. I like being able to use a research library, not to mention the convenience of being able to work out in the gym during lunch.

Ultimately, though, when you ask people why they choose to live among academics, you tend to hear the same answer: You get to hang around with really smart people. I used to respond the same way but was caught up short when I recently asked a friend, a well-established San Francisco money manager, what he liked about his job. His answer: You get to hang around with really smart people.

I love coming to work on this beautiful Gothic campus. In late summer the grounds are green and lush, wisteria dripping from above. I'm settling into my new office. The admissions building was formerly the home of the university president, so it has a very unofficey feel to it. Lots of differently shaped rooms, leaded windows. Not a Dilbert kind of space at all. And it's only a five-minute walk to the center of campus—not far to go for an intellectual fix and a latte with academic friends.

Since there are six of us starting out, being the new person is very easy. We're all deposited into our offices and given stacks of materials. We are instructed to spend the next few days reading. There's a new-staff manual that goes over some basic information: the general duties of an admissions officer and what is expected. There are lists of frequently asked questions. There are statistics.

We're told that we will be sitting in on various activities, primarily group information sessions, interviews, and on-call duty. There are ten admissions officers (four returning and the six new people) and four associates. These are the people responsible for reading the fourteen thousand applications submitted each year. We all have regional responsibilities. While interviewing I had stated my preference for recruiting in northern California. As it turns out, that region was available.

But they also wanted me to read Massachusetts, the state with the greatest number of elite private secondary schools. It's a hard sell, getting those boarding-school and private-day-school kids to think beyond the Northeast, beyond the Ivy League. A school like Duke, although the top choice for many kids from the South, just doesn't hold the same appeal to the snobbier Northeastern kids. That I was from New York, had lived in Manhattan, and perhaps most important, had gone to Yale, were reasons I was asked to handle Massachusetts.

The backgrounds of the other admissions officers are different from mine. Most of them are in their mid-to late twenties, a full decade and more younger than I. Of the returning staff, only one had gone to Duke. That's partly why three of the newly hired folks are alumni. The others have gone to far less selective schools. Two have had experience in admissions, again, at less selective schools. One of the Dukies, Victoria, recently dropped out of a Ph.D. program. Another, Chuck, graduated from the university only a year before but spent the intervening time doing research in a lab. The last seems to have some kind of vague teaching credential.

Of the four veteran officers, one is charged with doing African American recruiting, another with paying special attention to the Latino applicants. There is Missy, the career admissions person who had interviewed me ("How can you argue with them—they wrote the textbook!"), and Audrey, who went to a small but good liberal arts school and had fallen into a job in admissions a few years before. None of the associates had gone to elite schools.

The group information sessions are offered twice daily in the summer. An admissions officer, randomly assigned by the person who makes up the weekly schedule, leads them. The way new people are trained to do the "group" is by sending them off to listen to others. My first two weeks I listened to about five people do the group. I heard five distinctly different versions of Duke. Who gives the information session determines, to a large extent, what and how visitors think of the school.

There seemed to be two main goals. The first was to describe the school in a way that made it seem appealing and exciting. The second half of the program was to explain the admissions process in a way that was true and yet didn't discourage anyone from applying. If you gave the actual statistics about who, when all is said and done, gets into highly selective schools, people would walk away not only discouraged, but disgusted.

Each person's group was, not surprisingly, a reflection of her personality. The associate who had interviewed me—who had come from the college counseling side of the desk—tended to be very school-teachery. Her group was full of information, and a little short on enthusiasm. Audrey's group focused on things she thought were cool, such as the study-abroad programs in which one could go on archaeological digs, and the Sky Devils, the school's skydiving team. She took pleasure in giving certain statistics: because there was a 7,700-acre research forest at the school that gave it a ratio of 1.5 acres per student. While she gave the group, she smiled the whole time. She hating giving the group, I learned later. She'd be willing to swap a whole day of on-call duty just to get out of a one-hour group.

I had to come up with my own take on how to sell the school. Out of each group I listened to I found things that I could crib; I would make them my own later. We started giving the groups before going through the process of reading applications, so when I talked about admissions, I had very little idea of what I was talking about. I'd be asked questions that I could not answer. For the first few weeks, a seasoned admissions officer was sent along to help out the rookies; after that, we were on our own.

The information sessions in the summer are huge—more than a hundred warm bodies. In addition to making the group feel impersonal and performative, this is difficult because within the office there is no space large enough to accommodate all the visitors. So we have to move the group to a bigger room on campus. People show up early and settle into the living room of the admissions office, a comfortable space with a few sofas and overstuffed chairs and a lot of straight-backed less comfortable stacking chairs. And then the admissions officer announces to all those comfortably ensconced (and to the others standing anxiously in the lobby, seatless) that they will have to follow her for a "quick" walk up to campus to a more accommodating space. The walk takes about ten minutes. If it is extremely hot, or worse, raining, by the time you get them all into the larger room they hate you. I dreaded doing the group when it was raining. No matter how lively or enthusiastic you are, they hate you.

You learn quickly that each group somehow manages to take on its own personality. There were days when I was on: funny, smart, warm, and welcoming. And I played to an audience of sullen faces. Then there were the days when I stumbled. I'd forget things. My jokes would bomb. And yet, at the end, they would applaud wildly, coming up afterward to tell me what a good job I'd done, that mine was the best presentation they'd seen at any college. I found that it was easier and more fun to do the 10:00 A.M. group rather than the 2:00 P.M. one.

These families would spend weeks traveling around from college to college. On Tuesday afternoon they'd come to Duke having spent the morning at Chapel Hill. The day before they'd looked at Wake Forest, and Wednesday they'd go to the University of Virginia. By the afternoons, people were bushed. Sometimes they would have taken the campus tour before the group. At many schools there is a substantial content overlap between the admissions officer's information session and the student-led tour; students who work for the admissions office as tour guides (unpaid, at Duke) tend to see themselves as part of the admissions staff and like to volunteer answers to all sorts of questions, regardless of whether they actually know the answers.

The tour guides in the summer tended to be less-stellar students. They are around because they are taking the courses they couldn't fit in during the rest of the school year. Perhaps they are premeds, worried about lowering their GPAs and want to take organic chemistry in the summer as a stand-alone course. Or they are varsity athletes who didn't take a full course load during the semester because of practice. Or they are local kids, who'd rather hang out at Duke than with their families. The kids who choose to become tour guides are the ones who love the school, who feel lucky to be there. Often, they *are* lucky to be there, having been admitted for reasons other than their academic prowess.

Usually it was parents, rather than applicants, who raised their hands to ask questions at the end of information sessions. Once, after three long weeks of travel, deciding to experiment, I told an audience in northern California that we pay attention to who asks the questions, to whether it's the applicant who calls us, or their parent. The parents won't, after all, be the ones taking the calculus tests or writing the term papers on *Paradise Lost*. That evening only one parent came up at the end of the session to talk to me. I wished I'd figured out that little trick earlier in my admissions career.

In my first few weeks I sat in on interviews with the experienced admissions officers. Doing interviews was straightforward. What wasn't straightforward was how they figured into the process. The kids all seemed to think they needed them. So did their parents. In the summer, there would be two admissions officers each doing four interviews a day.

I realized soon why there was so much confusion about them: different schools use them differently. At Duke they are neither required nor evaluative. They are mostly there for public-relations purposes. Of the fourteen thousand or so students who apply each year, we are able to interview only about one thousand of them on campus. They tend to be those who can afford to make the trip. They tend to be, on the whole, the weaker portions of the applicant pool. For everybody else, if they send in part 1 of their application by December first (part 1 is their name, address, and sixty-dollar application fee—even if they don't bother to send in the rest of the application by the January second deadline, even if they never send it in at all, if we have their part 1 we get to count them in our applicant numbers) they will be offered an alumni interview. Someone who lives in their area who went to Duke— maybe three years ago, maybe thirty—will interview them.

Some kids interview on campus and then also request an alumni interview. They seem to think this will help them. There is good reason to feel this way. At some places, interviews—and other contacts with the school—are important. If you want to get into a small, elite liberal arts college, the best thing you can do is to make friends with your admissions officer. From what I under-stand, these schools do pay attention to the interviews and even track the number and kinds of contact that each applicant has with the school: if they've visited, if they've interviewed, and so on. Nobody wants to be a safety school. When you're admitting such a small class you want to be sure that each student who applies will come if accepted.

At Duke, however, it simply doesn't matter: there's no tracking. From a veteran admissions officer I learned to interview a kid and not bother to write up the conversation. We were supposed to write a brief description of what took place, note strengths and weaknesses, and then give a rating. Only in the rare cases in which I thought a student was fabulous would I bother to write it up. Or when a kid behaved in a particularly loathsome manner. Victoria interviewed a young man whose family name appeared on one of Duke's buildings. He came into her office for the interview, stretched out on the couch with his feet extended in front of him, and laced his fingers behind his head. He was, Victoria wrote, "the most arrogant young man I have ever encountered." She made sure that the interview report got into his file.

I sit in on my first interview. Alexis has come to campus having been home only four days from a trip to Paris. She is exquisitely and expensively dressed in a pearl-pink linen sheath. Her shiny WASP-straight hair is pulled into an elegant bun, her makeup simple, emphasizing her natural beauty. She talks at length about the art she had seen in Paris and displays a sophisticated nonchalance about her travels. The associate who is doing the interview asks Alexis about the trip, focusing in on the sponsorship. Was this school related? Did she go to France to study? Was she staying with a family? No. It seems that her family had taken this trip together. Every summer they rent a house in some European city and "get to know the culture." Alexis was, it turned out, a child of privilege. We ask about her family. "We're very involved in philan-thropy" she says, the "we" echoing through the room. What about your relationship to your family, we ask. "I've been off at boarding school for most of my life, so summers are the times that we spend together," she answers. When we inquire about her aca-demic interests, they don't seem to extend beyond art history. "My board scores aren't very high," she volunteers. "We're working on getting them up. I have a private tutor. I have a hard time with math. I haven't been able to get much above a six hundred on the SAT, even though I've taken it four times already. Do you think that will be a problem?"

After she leaves we discuss her candidacy. I think, no way. Wrong. I am told she'll likely be a development admit. I don't yet understand.

They come dressed in suits and ties, in khakis and torn T-shirts. Young women, especially in the summer, will wear spaghetti-strap tank tops and teeny tiny miniskirts. Some students have had a lot of experience talking to grown-ups, and about themselves, and it's a pleasure to converse with them. When I met Anna, from Los Angeles, we actually had a spirited exchange about the differences between the book and movie versions of Catch-22. Then there are shy farm girls from Iowa who won't make eye contact and look as if they are about to burst into tears at any moment because of sheer nervousness.

They tend to answer our questions in the same way; in ways that are both true and do nothing to make them stand out. What's your defining quality? I'd ask. Ninety-nine times out of a hundred the answer would be "I'm a perfectionist," or "I work really hard."

Of course you do. You wouldn't be applying to a school like this if you didn't. But what makes you different from all of the other hard workers? They don't realize how similar to all the other applicants they sound, and if you try to push them, they struggle feeling put on the spot and uncomfortable.

I was interviewing a dull boy. It was one of those excruciating times when he kept giving long canned responses to my questions. He had clearly rehearsed this interview many times. It was mind numbing. Finally I asked him to tell me something quirky or unusual about himself, something that would help me to remember him. This dull boy thought for a moment and said, "My nickname is Snickers." "That I'll remember," I said. A month later, before the applications were due, a huge box was delivered to me. I didn't recognize the name on the return address. When I opened it, there was a gross of Snickers bars with a note: "I wanted to make sure you still remembered me." It was signed "Snickers."

I did indeed remember him. It helped his application not in the slightest.

Chuck interviewed a kid whom he began to refer to as the "kid from Alabama with orange hair." Initially put off by the clearly dyed carrot-topped Southerner, after a few minutes of conversation Chuck said that this was the most impressive kid he'd ever met. Their talk ranged from music to philosophy to race relations in the South. "The Kid with Orange Hair" became the standard, in the office, for a great interview.

My least favorite of the in-house duties turns out to be on call. Each day an admissions officer is assigned the task of answering all the random phone calls that come into the office. We learn by listening to our colleagues, to one side of the phone call. "No," Audrey says, "we don't give out a median SAT score. What I can tell you is that the middle fifty percent of students admitted last year scored between 1350 and 1520." She listens. "Well," she says, patiently, "you are below the middle fifty percent. But that shouldn't stop you from applying. Standardized test scores are just one of the things we look at in considering your application." She puts down the phone. It rings again. "No," she says, "we don't give out a median SAT score."

The first time I was on call and I got an elementary school question I was horrified. "We have just moved to Durham," says the mom. "Which elementary school should we send our son to if we want to get him into Duke?" What became more horrifying to me was the frequency of this kind of question. "How can I best prepare my second grader for the SAT?" It's possible, I wanted to say, that by the time your second grader is ready to apply to college that class-biased test, which gives us little insight except perhaps into family income, will be abolished. We will have evolved to looking in more interesting, more complex ways, at seventeen-year-olds. My brother went to Bowdoin College because they didn't require the SAT. Mount Holyoke has just thrown it out. Will the Ivy League and other highly selective schools ever be so enlightened? Probably not. I don't say this but instead mutter some kind of vague answer about learning vocabulary.

On call I fielded Dad calls. Dads tend to recite the list of achievements of their child first, before they get to any kind of question. "She's very impressive," he'll say. "Has 1410, is in the top ten percent of her class—and it's a very competitive high school—she's captain of field hockey and president of the debate club. You're going to want her," he'll say. And I'm already thinking, poor kid, she probably doesn't have a chance of getting in, and waiting for his question. Which turns out to be something like, should she take AP statistics, which he thinks would be useful, or music theory, which is what she wants to take? Let her take what she wants to take. Will that help her get in?

Sometimes parents call wanting an honest assessment of their child's chances. "He's wanted to go to Duke for years, since watching Christian Laettner hit "the shot" on TV. But I'm worried that he's not going to get in and will be disappointed." She'll rattle off some facts about his candidacy—test scores, grades, extracurriculars. I tell her that although there's no way of knowing his chances without seeing an application, in my candid assessment, for what it's worth, it doesn't sound likely. If they're already worried about their chances, it's likely that they're not going to be competitive. Thank you, she says (I think sincerely), that's what I thought.

Now, from Duke's perspective, I have not given the "right" answer. The reason we do recruiting is to get the BWRKs to apply so that we can deny them and bolster our selectivity rating. We do not say this. Deans and directors of admissions publicly bemoan the competition among high school students for places at their prestigious institutions. They worry that kids are trying too hard, not able to enjoy their time in high school for the résumé-padding activities that they think they must have to look good to these schools. What they don't say, however, is that while the pool of "qualified" applications has grown enormously, the number of colleges to which they aspire and the number of places for admitted students has remained static. Although it's sweet that these admissions professionals worry about the regular good kids who are stressing themselves out, they're still not going to admit all those BWRKs.

The other duty of being on call is that you are also responsible for answering random E-mails that come into the "AskDuke" account. Kids write long, heartfelt E-mails, giving their credentials, pledging their bona fides, and expressing their desire to attend Duke, and somewhere, embedded in this linguistic mess, would be a question. The on-call officer was responsible for answering the question; the response came from the "AskDuke" account. As in all things, we each answered in our own image. Victoria would compose lengthy replies, giving lots of relevant information in a warm but didactic fashion. Dave's were muddled messes, offering not only useless but at times factually incorrect answers in incoherent sentences. Chuck's, on the other hand, were filled with detailed bits of information and helpful advice. Mine sucked—when I remembered to do them.

The last duty that I must master in my first month of work is planning my fall travel. There's been a lot of talk about "school visits" and "Duke nights." I'm not sure what a school visit is or which schools I'm supposed to visit. I'm given a large printout of "search numbers." This is a database of kids who have either scored above a certain point on their boards or have expressed an interest in our school. It's a way of trying to figure out which high schools will be worth visiting. We look for those where there are lots of "high-ability" kids and lots of folks who seem to be interested in hearing from us. Silly kids: They think that if they hear from us they have a better chance of getting in.

I look at the printout, which is broken down by high school, in zip code order. I notice that some of the schools that I have heard of, schools that have the reputation of being the best in the country, have low search numbers. I ask an associate about this.

"Oh that's because the college counselor tells them not to report their scores. She doesn't want them to be inundated with mail from colleges."

"So you can't go by these numbers?"

"Well, no, not really."

What most admissions people end up doing, then, is visiting the same schools each year. I have been given the itineraries for the past three years of the people who worked on my two areas, Massachusetts and northern California. The visited schools are a mix of elite private schools and public schools in affluent areas. The suburbs of Boston are rich with these kinds of places. Geographically I'm at a bit of a loss, particularly in northern California. While I can find the towns on the map, I can't tell how long it will take to travel from one to the next. I end up following the same itineraries that had been followed in previous years.

Since there are six of us new people, we form a sort of freshman class of our own. It's an easy, collegial office, though quite hierarchical. Above us, the "officers," are the associates, most of whom have been working in college admissions for more than a decade, most of whom have children of various ages. They seem rather removed from the experience of the applicants. As at many offices of admission, the majority of staff members are women.

The associates report to a senior associate director, who in turn reports to the director. As at many offices of admission, the director is a man.

The director is the public face of admissions, and it is he, rather than his staff, who meets with faculty and administrators when such meetings are called for. He is also the only person to speak with the press. We are told in our first week that if ever we receive a request for an interview, or get a call from a newspaper, we are to say nothing and to forward the call to the director's secretary.

In addition to our regional responsibilities, each of us has office duties as well. One person is in charge, for example, of the volunteer student tour guides. Another is responsible for putting together Blue Devil Days, the program for admitted students, in April, while someone else heads up the post-decision processing nightmare that occurs after we make decisions and then have to mail them out to anxious applicants. There are people on the staff whose job it is to run the computer systems, but they are strangely ineffectual, and Chuck ends up coordinating computer needs.

Each week a schedule for the following week is produced. Officers are assigned duties: the group information sessions, interviews, and on call. We are expected to log into a notebook any meetings that we have scheduled so that there will be no conflicts when the weekly schedule is issued. It is prepared by the supervisor of the phone room, a small, dark, and overheated room just off the reception lobby, where three African American women sit and answer the phones all day long. I like these women, and I particularly like the supervisor, who is a smart-mouthed, sometimes trash-talking, feisty woman my own age. She has a big thing for the movie *Gone with the Wind*, which amuses me even as I find it bizarre. In time, because of our friendship, when she makes up the weekly schedule she takes into account what she knows to be my preferences. For this reason, I am almost never assigned to be the officer on call.

We talk a lot about the racialized atmosphere of the place, not just Duke (which many of the African American employees of the university refer to as "the Plantation") but also of the admissions office. The workplace is divided into "professional" staff, meaning the admissions officers, and "operations" staff, meaning everyone else. The race divide is clear. And class rage and resentment simmers just below the nicely appointed surfaces.

Indeed, one of the things that strike me about my colleagues, the other "professionals," is the lack of diversity in their socioeconomic backgrounds. They come from well-heeled families; it shows in the shoes they wear, the clothes they buy. Or, that their parents buy for them. My professional peers are twenty-somethings. The women on the associate level are closer to my age, but I have taken an entry-level position. The people I end up socializing with are from another generation. When I meet colleagues from other admissions offices, the divide between younger staff and career admissions people seems frequently to be replicated.

One thing they seem to have in common though, is that they take their jobs seriously and they love their school. The notion of, if not blind, at least vision-impaired institutional loyalty to a place (because it admitted you, because it employs you) is a stretch for me.

Nor does it seem to me that the endeavor on which we are all embarked, recruiting and then selecting a class of students, is particularly difficult or serious. It is the business of educating students once enrolled—deciding which skills they should be developing, which ideas they should be exposed to, rocking their worlds, both intellectually and socially—that seems important. But that's not what we're here to do.

And so, even before I'd finished my first month in the office, I knew that I was going to be something of an outsider. Though I would do my best to create enthusiasm and excitement about Duke among the students I spoke with, nonetheless I would read with a bias freely acknowledged—we all like people just like ourselves—and I knew, unlike many of my more hardworking and earnest colleagues, that admissions was not going to be my next career.

I was, however, looking forward to hitting the road.

2

The Auroras of Autumn: *On the Road*

Having left my job as an editor of scholarly books, but having stayed on the fringes of the scholarly world, and given who I am, I can't avoid dating academics. That is both good and bad.

Academics have lots of free time. Not being on the nine-to-five daily grind means that they are frequently free to take the afternoon off to go for a hike, or to have a picnic, or to stop by the office where you are working a nine-to-five job. "Let's go on a long bike ride Thursday afternoon," they say. "Well, I'd love to, but [firmly] I HAVE TO WORK." Then they ask you again the next week.

Academics have no free time. Nearly every moment not spent working is a moment spent in anxiety about not working. The distinction between work time and free time is meaningless in the minds of most academics I know. Which means that, when their work is not going well, you're faced with an anxiety-ridden, depressed person who feels like a failure. When work is going swimmingly, you never see them.

When I worked in scholarly publishing, I enjoyed being able to dabble in the disciplines and, especially, to go to different academic conferences. But I was there to work. As the partner or date of an academic, you get to go to conferences and play. I actually like academic conferences, especially when they are on topics far afield from anything I know anything about. Nothing like a good paper on string theory to send me into intellectual ecstasy.

In fact, I've found that I'm more interested in dating scientists than humanities folks. I suspect that I may have a bit of the been-there-done-that when it comes to disciplines I've published. I like dating to be about expanding my world. One of my best first dates was with Andrew, who teaches medicine, but should have gone into physics. "Explain quantum mechanics to me, briefly and without resorting to equations," I demanded over dinner. He did, and I fell in love.

Academics also tend not to be overly materialistic. In one of my forays into dating outside of the professoriate, I was shocked by the emphasis on worldly possessions. Don't get me wrong—I like nice things as much as the next gal, but it's still kind of reassuring that I can count on one hand the number of academics I know who wear Armani.

On the other hand, having to explain why it's good to have shirts in more than one color can be a bit tiresome. And, at the risk of venturing into the realm of extreme stereotyping here—and having already confessed a predilection for science geeks—I must also add that it can be awkward having to deal with the substandard attention to personal hygiene that you sometimes find among academics. A few weeks after Andrew thrilled me with his talk about small things moving very quickly, I gave him a little disquisition of my own, extolling the virtues of using deodorant. Just before we moved in together, I went through his closet and helped him throw out every shirt with an ink stain on the pocket. That decimated his wardrobe, but his geek status remained, happily, unthreatened.

For better or worse, I am drawn to academics. Although I've never wanted to be one, they are the folks I like to be around. So, if you know someone I.S.O. a D.W.F., a man with the mind of a Feynman, the body of an Adonis, and the sense of humor of a David Lodge, send him my way.

My personal life in Durham has been put on hold. I tell friends who want to get together for dinner and men who have called for dates that I will be traveling for most of October. It's fairly easy for me to take off like this, much harder for my colleagues who are the mothers of young children. All of us, from the brand-new admissions officers to the director, do four to seven weeks of travel a year, mostly in the fall. Duke spends a lot of money on these trips. We're trying to get our applications numbers up.

I am driving through the fall foliage of the New England countryside, trying to locate the Calhoun School. Quaint little towns, with quaint little town squares, they're all starting to look the same. I'm struggling with the map and my directions when, at a break in the stone wall along this country road, I see a sign. The Calhoun School.

No college rep ever visited my high school, a public school in upstate New York. This is the case for the majority of high schools in this country. However, there are a number of schools that are preyed upon by colleges of all sorts. Visits are scheduled months in advance. Students sign up, either because they're interested in hearing about the school or there's a class that they want to get out of. It's not hard to spot the college reps in the context of high schools. They tend to be older than the students and to dress better than the teachers. They have a harried look, having just come—late—from another school, and are already watching the clock knowing that they'll be late to their next appointment.

Generally a rep visits four or five schools a day. There's a lot of driving between schools; even if it's not far, there's a good possibility of doubling or tripling your travel time by getting lost in the residential neighborhoods in which these schools are rumored to be found. After the last school visit of the day, you have a little time to relax, perhaps eat dinner, and then it's on to the next event, meeting with alumni or an evening program.

I arrive at Calhoun on time. It's usually difficult to park at these schools, but here I'm lucky to find an unoccupied visitor spot. The place feels like a small New England college. It's breathtakingly beautiful. I go through the enormous doors into the main administrative building and am met by two obese black Labrador retrievers. They pant and slobber an enthusiastic hello.

I accost a student walking down the hallway.

"College counseling?"

"Oh, just down the hall and to the left, and then—hey, I'll take you there." These kids are used to us coming into their world, and, savvy about the admissions process, they often pant and slobber like the labs.

"What school are you from?" my guide asks me. She is wearing slim-fitting exquisitely tailored black pants and a short-sleeved cashmere turtleneck, also black. She is extremely thin, and my guess is that the Upper East Side of Manhattan is her home address.

I tell her.

"Oh, wow," she says, "that's my first choice school. I'm Claire. Claire Hess. I'll be at your presentation."

We've arrived at the counseling office, and a large woman wearing a jumper and a grosgrain headband is waiting for us to wrap up our conversation.

"I see you've already met one of your kiddies," she says, holding out her hand and introducing herself as Becky, director of college counseling. "Claire wants to apply early decision to Duke."

"That's wonderful," I say, and thank Claire for her help. "I guess I'll see you shortly."

"You sure will."

I'm whisked through a large room plastered with posters and pennants from colleges around the country. There are notices reminding students of the sign-up dates for the SAT, and I spot a posting letting them know that first drafts of their essays are due in the college counseling office the following week. I find myself wondering how much help these kids are getting in writing their essays.

I follow Becky down the hall, and we go into her office, a sun-drenched warm, inviting place. Becky herself is warm and inviting.

"So, this is your first year reading our kids," she says.

"Yep. Can't wait."

"Well, I think you should know that this is a very special school.

37

Our students are quite extraordinary, and our faculty, well, our faculty is truly outstanding. They expect a lot from the kids. And the grading here is—well, they haven't heard of grade inflation. So when you're reading our folders, you're not going to see a whole lot of As."

"You mean, you have no A students here?"

"Very few. But they tend to stay in the Northeast. You probably won't be seeing their applications."

I'm getting the picture. We will see only the second tier of this school. Fine, but they're probably not going to be admitted.

Suddenly, an older gentleman appears in the doorway.

"Is this the new Duke person?" he asks, making his way into the office and taking a chair across from me.

"Ben, I'd like you to meet our new rep," says Becky. I can tell that she's not thrilled to see him here.

"So what's the deal with K. becoming A.D.?"

"Excuse me?"

"K. Why A.D.? Why now?" He's looking at me like I'm a complete moron.

"I'm sorry, but I'm not following you."

Oh God, I suddenly realize. This is basketball talk. He means Coach K. A.D.? Athletic director?

"I'm sorry I don't really know much about basketball."

Now he's looking at me like I'm a moron from another planet.

"And they let you work there? Christ. Well, how's my old friend Claudia?"

"Claudia?"

"Isn't Claudia still out there in the file room? She used to bring in lunch for everyone."

Becky intervenes. She explains that some time ago Ben spent two months as a visitor in our office in which he was working as a faux admissions officer, in order to better understand our process. Since then he has been Calhoun's expert on Duke. He has, he tells them, the inside track on how we do admissions.

"So, when exactly were you there?"

"I read applications in 1980 for Duke."

I see. Now I'm getting it.

"Gee," I say. "That's when I applied to college."

"Did you go to Duke? Perhaps I read your application."

"I did not. Didn't even think of applying to Duke back then. Wasn't even on my radar screen. In fact, when I took this job I asked my college roommate—from Yale—if she'd ever considered applying to Duke. She said, "Oh yes, it was my safety school." Our selection process has changed quite a bit since you were with us."

His face has tightened, and he is glaring at me. He mutters something about needing to get to class and quickly departs.

Becky looks embarrassed, and I realize why we never see good applicants from this school. It's going to be a long trip.

Next I'm moving on to Berkeley Academy, about twenty-five minutes through the hills and dales of this part of Massachusetts. When I get there I see kids hanging out on the quad in grungy clothes. I see kids with green hair. Magenta hair. I also end up seeing no kids at all. No one has expressed an interest in hearing about Duke. The college counselor explains that their kids are, well, too cool for Duke. They go to schools like Brown, and Reed, and Oberlin, and UC Santa Cruz. A preppy jock school like Duke just doesn't do it for them.

The counselor and I end up having a nice chat. Turns out he, too, is a runner, and we talk races, PRs, and shoes for a while. And then I'm on my way.

Next stop, the Jonathan Edwards School. Another beautiful campus. Another set of overweight dogs.

I see a roomful of eager kids. Shiny happy people. They ask lots of questions about athletics; don't seem too interested in the academic portion of our program. They all try to make sure I remember their names and little tidbits about them. "What's your pottery program like?" I'm asked by a kid from LA with a nose ring, who later turns out to be the not terribly bright daughter of a very famous movie star. "Do you know the name of the field hockey coach?" A short Asian girl asks, "What's the median SAT?" They are polite and charming.

After the bell has rung the secretary tells me that Dana wants to see me, so I'm shown into the college counselor's office and sit and wait for a while. It's not bad, actually, to just sit.

"Well, hello there. I'm Dana. So lovely to meet you." She's tall and elegantly gray.

She interrogates me on my pedigree, starting with where I went to high school. Not impressed. But she seems pleased that I went to Yale. She waxes enthusiastic when I tell her about my former publishing career.

"I'm an author," she tells me.

I ask.

Turns out she has written three mystery novels. Still looking for "just the right publisher," she says.

She asks me what I read, and we have a brief conversation about current fiction. I'm furtively checking my watch.

Finally she says, "Well, I suppose I should tell you about our school."

I nod and smile.

"This is a wonderful place and our students are most remarkable. They are deliciously creative and work harder than students at any other school, I'd venture to say. Our grading system is extremely rigorous, our faculty unrelentingly demanding. Plus all of our kids are expected to take part in athletics, so they don't really have any free time here. When you're reading our files, if you have questions, and I'm sure you will, as this is your first year, though I must say that you are certainly one of the most intellectual admissions officers I have ever had the pleasure to meet, please do call me for help."

As I'm leaving, she hands me a school profile. It's a significant tool, useful in decoding a school's academic rigor and grading system. I look at it briefly. The first thing I notice is the matriculation of the previous year's class. At an expensive boarding school like this one, I would have expected to see far more students going to highly selective colleges and universities. There were no more than a few at Princeton, Dartmouth, and Penn. None to Harvard, Yale, Stanford, or Duke.

What caught my eye was the breakdown of the class. Although most of these schools refuse to rank their students, they usually give us some way to tell where a student stands within the context of their class. Jonathan Edwards School breaks its students into groups, with group 1 the top of the class, group 4 the bottom. Out of eighty-nine students, fifty-seven were in group 1. We generally don't take students outside of the top 5 percent of the class. We usually don't take them outside of the top two or three places. At Jonathan Edwards we would be given no real way to know which students were doing the best work. "Deliciously creative."

On my second day of travel I'm hitting the public schools in the greater Boston area. I am staying in Cambridge, where I thought it would be nice to hang out in the evenings. But by the time evening came around last night I was exhausted. I took a bubble bath, got into bed, and watched cable TV. Actually, I watched the channels whizzing by as I tried to find something to watch that would hold my interest. I fell asleep around 9:30.

This morning traffic is snarled all the way up the highway, and I realize that Cambridge was probably not the most convenient location, after all. I have the map out to get to the high school and reach my destination with about three minutes to spare.

I park and try to find the main entrance. It's not as easy as it might seem. Finally I enter the building and begin my search for the college counseling office. Except that here it's not called college counseling, it's called the career center. I come into a room that is lined with posters from colleges across the country. There are some beautiful posters here, from colleges I've never heard of. It seems there's an inverse relationship between the prestige of the school and the elegance of their marketing materials. I never saw any of the ugly Duke posters hanging in these offices. Nor did I see Harvard's, Princeton's, or Yale's.

Carol, a gracious and professional woman, who introduces herself as the head of the career center, meets me. She leads me into a room; around the table are a dozen kids. I thank her, sit down at the table, and begin passing out the cards on which I ask the kids to fill out their name, address, high school, and Social Security number.

"What if I don't want to put my Social Security number down?" asks a guy with a baseball hat turned backward on his head.

"That's fine. It's just an easy way for us to keep track of you. If you end up coming to Duke, it will serve as your student ID number."

"Yeah," says the guy sitting next to him, "like you're going to be going to Duke. Get real."

"What if I already visited?" asks a girl with long black curls. "Do I still need to fill out the card?"

"Yes, unfortunately, you do," I tell her. What I don't tell her is that it's so we can broadly, though not individually, track the contact we've had with kids, to try to figure out how many kids who visit end up applying, and of those, how many we admit and how many matriculate. And the same thing for school visits. We do these things to convince ourselves that we're collecting data.

Once all the cards have been filled out and passed back to me I arrange them in front of me corresponding to each kid. In that way I can try to put faces with the names.

"How many of you have already visited the campus?" Nine of them raise their hands.

"Wow. So," I say, "what questions do you have at this point?"

"How do you get in?" asks the kid with the hat.

Cutting right to the chase. "Okay, here's the deal. The way I think about getting into a highly selective school is that it's like competing in a decathlon. How do you win a decathlon?" They look at each other blankly. "Do you have to win every event," I ask? No, they shake their heads. "No," I say. "You have to win a couple of events. You have to be pretty darn good at all of them, but if there are some where you're really strong, that can compensate for weaknesses in other areas. So we look at you in six events (not ten, I say, but if I'd said it's like competing in a sexthalon you might have gotten the wrong idea). You have to be pretty darn good in all of them. But if you have some real strengths, say in extracurriculars, that can make up for weaknesses in other areas, like standardized testing."

I believe this when I say it, but that's only because I haven't yet read any applications. I continue to say it during my time in admissions, knowing that it's not exactly true. But it is what people want to believe. I'd like to believe it.

"We get about fourteen thousand applications each year for an entering class of sixteen hundred students. Each application is read twice: by a first reader, and then by an admissions staff member, a regional officer. We also have an African American recruiter and a Latino recruiter, and those applications get read a third time. Each regional officer is responsible for a section of the country—of the world. Your region is determined by where you go to high school, not by your home address. So boarding school students in Massachusetts, whose home may be Kentucky, are considered as applicants from Massachusetts and are read by me, the regional officer.

"I am your advocate. My job is to make the case to get you into Duke. Your job is to make my job as easy as possible by giving me a lot of ammunition to argue for you in selection committee.

"So, what do we look at? The first thing is curriculum choice. Which courses, of those available to you in your school, have you taken? If you're at a school, like this one, that offers twenty Advanced Placement Courses, we expect you to be taking advantage of some of them. If, on the other hand, you are applying from a school that doesn't offer any, we won't hold it against you. We are only concerned that you are taking the most rigorous curriculum available to you. We look at every grade you've received, starting in ninth grade. We note honors, Advanced Placement or International Baccalaureate, or college courses. We want you to be taking the most difficult load you can, without getting in over your head. And we ask ourselves what you've done with the opportunities available to you. Have you created ways to challenge yourself? Have you risen to the challenges you've set out?

"Separate, but related to curriculum choice, is achievement. Grades. The reason that it's separate but related can be seen from questions students, often juniors, ask, Should I take an easy course where I know I'll get an A, or a harder course, where it's possible my grade won't be as good? The answer is, of course, take the harder course and get an A. If you want to get into a good school." They laugh. I laugh.

"But we know that not all schools grade with the same standards. There are schools that give out virtually no As. And there are schools that have sixty-four valedictorians. So don't worry so much about your GPA, but concern yourself with taking hard classes and doing as well as you possibly can. It's true, the students that we admit tend to do very well in school, but they don't have to be perfect. Generally almost all of the students that we do admit are in the top ten percent of their class from public schools like this one, and from the top quarter of the elite private schools. Given that, the stronger the academic record, the better the chances of admission, but we don't feel compelled to take only the top few in each class.

"And, by the way, you're not competing with each other. We have no quotas—well, actually, just one but it doesn't apply to you. We're committed, by our charter, to keeping at least thirteen percent of our population from our home state of North Carolina. Other than that, we don't care where you're from, or which high school you attend. If all twelve of you apply and you all look good to us, we'll take you all. If none of you looks appealing (they giggle), we won't take any.

"Okay, next, yes, we do look at standardized testing. If you take the SAT, you need to take three SAT IIs [what used to be called achievement tests]. We don't care which subjects you take, but you must take three of them. If you take the ACT, you don't need any SAT IIs, at least not for Duke. Other schools require different permutations of these tests, and you should find out what the requirements are for the different schools to which you are applying. We no longer report an average SAT for our admitted students. That's because there's a hormone that, if it hears the average, causes a teenager to think in the following way: If I'm below the average, no way am I going to get in, and if I'm above it, no sweat. It doesn't work that way. So now we just report a middle fifty percent of admitted students. Do we admit people below the middle fifty percent? You bet. Do we deny those with double eight hundreds? Yep. Why? Because testing is just one factor, and while it does matter, it's not determinative. A high scorer with a mediocre class record looks like a lazy underachiever to us.

"We look at what people say about you. You need letters of recommendation from your college counselor and from two teachers. Sometimes, in small private schools, students get to know their college counselors very well, even have them as teachers. In large public schools there are applicants who have never personally met with their guidance counselor. That's fine. What we need to know from them is basic information about the school: the number of students in the class, the percent that go on to four-year colleges, the number of advanced courses offered, and so on. The more important recommendations are from your teachers. They must be in academic areas like math, science, history, or English, and they must have taught you in junior or senior year. If, and only if, there is someone who knows you well, and can help us understand things about you in a way that supplements what your teachers say, you may send in an additional recommendation.

"Just be judicious. Make sure that they know you *really* well and that they will say something different about you. The record in our office for additional recommendations is thirty-four. A colleague of mine, at Georgetown, told me that she had a student send in seventy-two additional letters of recommendations. Neither of those kids got in. In our file room there's a saying that's sort of mean, but also sort of true: the thicker the file, the thicker the kid. If you're padding your application with letters or with copies of every little prize you won since junior high school we're going to wonder if you think you're a weak applicant.

"The teacher recommendations, however, are crucial. The transcript does not speak for itself. While it will tell us what grades you've received, it won't tell us how hard you had to work for them or what kind of a contribution you made in the classroom. We look for students who are engaged in learning, who think about the material rather than simply spit it back by rote. It's better to ask a teacher in whose class you worked hard than one where you coasted to an easy A.

"We also look at what you do, how you spend your time. We look for well-rounded kids, but we also look for "well-lopsided" kids. If all you do is music—you don't do sports, you don't do community service, you don't do student government, you just do music—that's fine. We're trying to create a well-balanced class, that consists both of well-rounded people and of those who are more focused. We look for impact and for commitment. Not just what you do, but how you've done it and for how long. To stand out in extracurriculars you can show spectacular achievement in one area, or outstanding prowess in several. There's no one right way to do it. If you don't do any extracurriculars because you work thirty-five hours a week, that's fine, too. We just want to know how you spend your time.

"Of those five areas, you'd be surprised at how similar many of our fourteen thousand applicants look. They've all taken hard classes, done well, their standardized testing is in the same ballpark, teachers say they're the greatest thing since sliced bread, and even extracurriculars start to look a lot alike—captain of three varsity sports, president of debate, National Honor Society member. So how do I remember my favorite applicants?"

They look at me, look at each other. "Essays," mutters someone. "What?" I say. "Essays," he repeats more loudly.

"Exactly. Essays. Here's the thing. At this point in senior year, your essays are the one part of the application that you have complete control over. They are your opportunity to communicate directly with the admissions officer reading your application—that would be me—who you are, how you think, what you care about. I make a couple of assumptions when I read essays" I say, before I've ever read one. "I assume that you will show your essay to someone else so that there will be no egregious grammatical errors, no embarrassing typos. So that the last line of your college application essay to Duke doesn't read, "And that's why I really want to go to Stanford." Someone else should look over your work and save you from yourself. I had a girl last year who wrote that she wanted to go to a 'smaller private school like Duke,' not one of the 'big state pubic institutions.'

"As far as I'm concerned, you can write about any topic you want. Nothing is off limits. It's not what you write about, but how you write about it. So if you care about your dog, write about your dog. If running is your life, write about running. But just make sure that no other runner could have written the same essay. Make sure that your personal statement is, well, personal.

"So that's what we look at when we're making our evaluations about whom to admit. There's no formula. We look at everything.

We read everything that you send in. We try to understand you as a person and as a student, and when it comes time to present your application to the selection committee, we end up talking about you as if we know you. You'd be amazed at how attached we can get to our applicants. You will find this an extremely, perhaps an excruciatingly, personal process. You'll feel like you're pouring your whole life onto these sheets of paper. And then what you'll think—isn't it amazing, that I know what you'll think, but I do—is that it will all go into some big institutional void and a big old computer will spit out a decision, yes or no, and that will determine where you go to college. What I want you to know is that this is an intensely personal process for the admissions officer as well. You are sending your application in not to a computer, but to me or to a person just like me. So I will comb through your materials and look for something that will help me present you as a compelling applicant to the selection committee.

"In April, after decisions have been released and students are visiting campus trying to decide where they want to go to school, you will find admissions officers patrolling the lobby of our building. They go up to kids and ask where they're from. 'Hey, Victoria,' I'll call out to one of my colleagues if a kid says he's from her region. 'Here's one of yours.' And she'll scurry over wanting to meet the person whose application she fell in love with.

"It's also a process that can be overwhelming. But you should realize that you have a lot of control. You make the decision where you want to apply to college. You travel around the country, collecting impressions of various schools. Realize that these impressions are subjective and are flawed. You may be influenced by a variety of factors. If it's a horrible rainy day, you may not like a particular campus. If you have a wonderfully perky tour guide, you may think—I want to go where she goes. If you have a boring admissions officer who talks for hours and says nothing interesting, you may be tempted to cross that school off your list. Remember that it is your job to flesh out these impressions with more information. Read our publications. Visit our Web sites. And most important, talk to current students. If you can, visit and stay overnight with a student. That's the best way to see if a school might be a good fit for you.

"Once you decide where you want to apply to college, you have more decisions. A big one is regular or early decision. For most schools, the regular decision deadline is January second. You will find out by early April. Then there is early decision. Early decision is binding. If you apply to an early decision school and are admitted, you must come. You will either be admitted, denied, or deferred. Different schools handle deferrals differently. At some schools, including Duke, almost no one is denied early. Most of the kids who apply are deferred, and most of them will be denied in April. Some schools, if they know they're not going to take you in April, will deny you early in order to encourage you to move on in your thinking. Early decision is a great option if you're sure about your first-choice school. It's a good option for two reasons. First, with luck, you can get the whole process out of the way and you can enjoy the spring of your senior year in high school. And because the admit rate for many schools is much higher if you apply early. At Duke, for example, we take a third of the class early decision. That means the admit rate is about forty percent. For regular decision, the admit rate is more like twenty percent. Is it easier to get in early? You do the math.

"Early decision is different from early action. Early action schools will tell you if you are admitted, but you are not committed to attending them. You can apply to an early decision school, like Duke, and an early action school, like Brown or Harvard. But if you're accepted to both, you're coming to Duke.

"Other factors that go into the selection are things like athletics—if you think you are recruitable to play a varsity sport, you should contact the coach directly, or have your coach contact our coach; geography—most schools look for geographic diversity without having set quotas; alumni or sibling ties—we like the children and siblings of people who attended our schools. Most selective schools give a little boost to legacy children, as long as their qualifications are within the ballpark of acceptable. What we say is that being a legacy can heal the sick, but it can't raise the dead. Unless, of course, you have dead (or living) relatives who have donated millions.

"We, like most highly selective colleges and universities, believe in creating a diverse community, which means diversity across a spectrum of factors: race, geography, class and socioeconomic background, religion, etc. We are firmly committed to Affirmative Action and seek to get the best students of color into our applicant pool and into our entering classes.

"We are also one of the few remaining need-blind schools. This means that we make our admissions decision regardless of the ability of the applicant to pay. We will meet full demonstrated need for those who apply for financial aid. "Demonstrated need," the financial aid office tells us, may be different from "want." What you want and what they think you need may not be the same thing. But Duke is committed to making it affordable, if not cheap, for everyone who gets in to be able to attend. And it's not cheap. Total costs are in excess of thirty-two thousand dollars a year. About half of our student body is on some kind of financial aid. Packages are built up from self-help, which includes low-interest loans and work-study jobs, and outright grants. The formulae aren't simple, but while Duke doesn't expect your family to liquidate all of its assets to pay for an education, it does expect you to have saved. Students are expected to earn money over the summer, and if they've saved for college, Duke expects them to use that money for their education. While the official line is that we don't negotiate or compare packages, the financial aid office does want to know everything about your financial situation that would help them to make Duke affordable to you. My best advice is to fill out all forms quickly and completely and get them back before the deadlines."

As an aside, I tell them that I am in my late thirties and have just now finished paying back my student loan.

"Okay," I take a breath. "Questions?"

A girl in a twin set raises her hand.

"What about the common application? I heard that if you don't use the school's own application, they'll think you're not really interested and will be less likely to accept you?"

"Good question, because that's a popular misconception. For the schools that use the common application, we all sign a sworn statement saying that we will not treat preferentially one kind over the other. So we don't care if you use our own app, the common app, or if you download either one and apply electronically. We just want you to apply. If you do use the common application, you must fill out the school's own supplement. It asks important questions like, have you ever been convicted of a felony, and it requires you to answer the Duke essay questions. So using the common application won't get you out of any writing, but it will save time filling out applications. If I were applying today, I would use the common app."

I glance at my watch and realize that not only am I out of time, but I am going to be late for the next school.

"Well, that's it," I say as begin to pack up my stuff. "I hope you all apply. And I'll look forward to reading your applications."

I rush out, scramble to find my car, and once I get onto the suburban streets get hopelessly lost looking for the next school.

Eventually I make my way to the Eliot School, a private school in downtown Boston. I get there and am met by two college counselors who want to see me before they introduce me to the two students anxious to hear my spiel.

"We wanted to show you their transcripts, first," says Meg, "to see if it was even reasonable to let them apply. They're both legacies, one at Penn, the other at Harvard. For Penn, they only give their legacies a boost if they apply early. We feel that it's Jon's best shot of getting in anywhere and want to encourage him to take it. But for some reason he's become fixated on Duke. Brent's not only a Harvard legacy, but there will be strong development interest in him. Have a look at their transcripts and you'll see the problem."

They hand me the transcripts. I look at them. I have no idea of what I'm supposed to be looking for. I see some Cs and Ds. That can't be good, but I have no idea what the grading structure at this school is like. I see honors classes listed, but I don't know if there are courses taught above the honors level. Basically I'm lost again.

"Well," I say, "since I haven't yet had experience reading applications, I'm a bit at a loss about what to tell you. You would know better than I, at this point, about how likely it would be for kids with transcripts like this to get into these schools. I'm really a rookie."

They thank me for my candor (what else could I do?) and tell me that the boys are very excited to meet me. They lead me into an outer office, where there are in fact two boys waiting anxiously.

"Hey," they both exclaim, and thrust forward their hands for me to shake. "You're the Duke lady." I guess I am. "Tell us about camping out for basketball tickets," they say. "I want to know about your Russian program," the little guy says. "I'm going to try to walk on to the football team," the big beefy one declares. "We love Duke," they say together. They are practically panting. Their enthusiasm is wonderful and amusing and I easily fall into the groove.

I have one more school to visit today, Ezra Stiles Prep, an all-male private school. I've never thought much about single-sex education. This will be a new experience. I'm led into a living room where there are a dozen boys sitting around in a circle. As soon as I enter the room, they all stand.

"Sit, sit," I say, and take a seat among them. They turn out to be a sweet group of boys, polite, well spoken, and they ask good and thoughtful questions. After we're through I am taken by one of them, a short Asian guy named Winston, to the office of the college counselor. We sit and chat and I like her immediately.

"This is a special school," Muffy says. Oh no, she's going to feed me the same old line.

"What we focus on here is character." What? I had sneaked a look at the school profile before I came. What I saw was that there are forty-eight boys in a class, from widely diverse backgrounds, since, as the school is one of the oldest and best endowed in the country, they have a lot of financial aid help available to students. The median SAT score was 1490. All of the boys in the class get into the best colleges and universities, Harvard taking the lion's share each year.

"The boys are smart and hardworking. But the emphasis here is on being a good person. Let me tell you a story that I think will give you a sense of what kind of place this is. Last year the headmaster pulled aside, individually, two boys. 'You're not being nice enough,' he told each of them. 'I want you to do one nice thing for a person every single day.' Since the headmaster runs the school with an iron fist, the boys were not in a position to refuse. After a couple of weeks one of the boys came up to him. 'I started helping my little brother with his homework because of the assignment you gave me,' he said. 'But what happened is that I've really gotten to know him. I actually like him. And I like myself better when I'm helping him.' That's what kind of a school this is."

I like this school.

3

Notes Toward a Supreme Fiction: *Describing Duke*

I spend about two hours every Sunday morning with people I almost never see fully clothed.

Rain or shine (I prefer shine), hellishly hot or bone-chillingly cold (I prefer hot), we gather in a parking lot just off Duke Forest to do a long run together. Many of us run solo six days a week. But Sundays we become a pack.

A little before eight, we start to arrive; often the more hard core have already jogged a few miles to warm up. You never really know who is going to show, but you know there'll be someone to run with for nine, or thirteen, or more miles. And I know that I can look forward not only to a bracing run but to bracing conversation on, among other things, local politics, affirmative action, the shortlist for the Booker Prize, college basketball, and academic gossip.

For most of my life, I was an anti-runner. In college, all of my friends jogged. When I lived in New York, my best friend never missed her morning six miles. Once, while I was on vacation with a friend and another couple, the three of them went out to run on the beach for an hour. I stayed and lounged on the deck in my black bikini, eating Oreos and reading a novel. I thought they were nuts.

It happened accidentally. I began running with Andrew, an academic psychiatrist, because I thought my dog needed more exercise. We started out with a three-mile loop around Duke's golf course, which is god-awful hilly. I couldn't run the whole way. At times, when faced with a big hill, I'd bark out, "Tell me about schizophrenia!" or "What the hell is serotonin, anyway?" A natural and amusing pedant, Andrew would then give me a minilecture that was so engrossing and diverting that we'd crest the hill before I knew it.

When I met Peter, I was transformed from a jogger to a runner. Peter, a zoologist, had been the women's-track coach at Duke in the dark days before Title IX. He's a great coach and a good runner. On our runs we've discussed the civil-rights movement, Quakerism, political correctness, science and the "science wars," Wittgenstein, mutual friends, books, music, film (though this is a man whose favorite movie is *Babe*, so we don't spend too much time on film), and have had some high-voltage arguments (often, it seems, just for the sake of arguing, since we basically agree on most things). It's never personal, and it's always stimulating. Our arguments tend to make us run faster; when we run with others, however, our companions often try to change the subject.

I am not a joiner. I joined a running club, even became an officer. And I started showing up, religiously, for the long runs on Sunday mornings.

The back of the Sunday pack is a wonderfully interesting place, and when I'm tired, I love to run with Walter, an epidemiologist. His work has taken him all over the world, and he manages to plug into the global network called the Hash House Harriers (bunches of people who describe themselves as "a drinking group with a running problem") wherever he is, be it San Francisco, Taiwan, or Copenhagen. Walter often runs with Jim, a pilot, whose dad was a statistics guru at UNC. Turns out that Walter and Jim, good buddies, had both been involved in a long-term relationship with the same woman (sequentially, not simultaneously). I know more about Louise than almost any other person I have never met.

Some people may consider a weekly Sunday-morning half-marathon as, at best, an exercise in self-punishment. Most of the academics I run with think of it as a luxury, along the lines of taking two hours over coffee. It's a necessary and fun part of their social lives. When else, I often ask myself, would I get a chance to see and talk to these people? Certainly not once a week, probably not once a month. But every Sunday, I get a window of privileged time, an opportunity to be with people I like, and respect, and admire, and learn from.

Today, after a long day of school visits, I run by myself along the Charles River, nodding hellos to the other runners and thinking about what I have to do tonight. I have scheduled a Duke Night, an evening program with a slide show to which we invite all juniors and seniors on our "prospect" list. Kids feel that if they're invited, they have to come. This misguided sentiment generally insures a sizable crowd. I've planned the event to take place at a hotel in

Newton, a location readily accessible via the two main highway arteries that go through Boston. I did this at the suggestion of our local alumni representative.

I trot back to my Cambridge hotel in time to shower and change into grown-up clothes and get back in the rental car. When I get there my helpful alum has already started checking out the room, setting up tables, getting ready. As we chat, an hour or so before the program is scheduled to begin, the first family arrives.

"Hi," says the mom. "We're here for the Duke thing."

"You're in the right place," I tell her. "We'll need the student to sign in; you can take some brochures and then make yourself comfortable. What school do you go to?" I ask her son.

"Lanshts."

"Excuse me?"

"Lansing High School," his mom chimes in. This is clearly a case where the child has been dragged along. He doesn't want to be here. His mom is filling out the sign-in sheet for him, and he's looking surly. It's going to be a long night.

Soon other families start to arrive. Then it's a nonstop stream. I'm meeting and greeting, smiling and welcoming. My face is starting to hurt from smiling. The room is filling up. There's a nervous energy. People are friendly, but tense. The kids shake my hands firmly. It's getting to be time to start the show. I'm a little nervous myself. Once I get started, I think, it'll be fine. It's just hard getting started.

I start by welcoming them, thanking them for coming. I make a joke about the traffic—and the traffic patterns—in Boston. They laugh. Thank God. I tell them what I'm going to be telling them.

First, I'll do a fifteen-minute slide show giving them some general information about Duke. Next, I'll talk a bit about admissions and financial aid. Finally I'll open the session up for questions. I nod the cue to my alum and he dims the light.

The big themes we are supposed to stress in our presentations are youth, academics, location, and spirit. The youth of the university is one of the things that make it distinctive. In 1924, with $40 million dollars of tobacco money, James Buchanan Duke decided to create a research university out of what was originally a small regional college. So unlike our peers (we considered our "peers" to be Harvard, Yale, Princeton, Stanford, and MIT—though I wondered if they ever mentioned Duke in the same breath), all of whom strive to establish priority, to be the oldest, we embrace the newness of Duke and argue that it makes us more interesting, less institutionally self-satisfied, less tradition bound, and more willing to try new things. This is sort of true.

"I consider Duke," I tell the good folks gathered here to hear me, "the Doogie Howser of American universities. We're a baby on the higher education scene. But in just seventy-five years we've managed to accomplish what it took our peer institutions a couple of centuries." They laugh. I wonder if Doogie Howser is still on TV or if I am hopelessly dating myself.

In promoting Duke we talk about academic opportunities as if the school had the teaching ethos of a small liberal arts college embedded in the facilities of a major research university. My guess is that this is exactly what all of the highly selective research universities say about their schools. We all boast a world-class faculty who does world-class research while remaining first and foremost committed to the teaching of undergraduates. I mention by name a number of faculty members whom I know make it a habit to invite their students into their homes for dinner. My friend John, I say, a historian lives in a first-year dorm with his wife, three kids, dog, and what he calls his "terrorist" cat. He spends a lot of time hanging out with the kids who live in his dorm. He'll have midnight breakfasts for them where he makes waffles and homemade toppings. He's gotten the award for best teaching, I say. What I don't tell them is that he has virtually no chance of getting tenure and will soon be kicked out of the university. Too much time teaching and hanging out with the students, not enough research and publishing.

I tell them that, yes, there are big lecture courses, but that's not necessarily a bad thing. "Something like forty percent of the freshman class takes introductory chemistry. Except that we don't call it chemistry. At Duke it's Bonkistry, and it's been Bonkistry for the forty years that Professor James Bonk has been teaching it. He's now teaching, he told me recently, the grandchildren of his first students. And he still teaches it with the same enthusiasm as he did when he started out. You may have heard of him. There's an urban legend, which turns out to be true, and revolves around a story about Jim Bonk.

"Four young men went off to spend the weekend at a nearby college. They had a bit too much to drink, and by the time Monday rolled around they were not prepared to take their chemistry exam. They went to their professor and explained that they had gone away for the weekend and on their way home, they got a flat tire. Could they possibly have an extension and take the test a week later?

"Professor Bonk thought about it and told them yes, that would be fine. When they showed up the next week he put them in four separate classrooms and gave them each the same test. It contained but two questions. The first was a straightforward chemistry question on the material they had just been studying. It was worth ten percent of the grade.

The remaining ninety percent of the grade for this test rested with the second question. It said, simply, 'Which tire?' "

I tell them that our faculty is extraordinary. They are the people doing the research, writing the books, and publishing the articles that set the academic agenda throughout the world. And they are teaching our undergraduates. "Every first-year student is required to take a seminar. You can take one of the fifty or so first-year seminars that are offered in the spring semester. These classes are limited to fifteen students, all freshmen, and are taught by the cream of the academic crop. The best-known professors are teaching our youngest students."

This is true. But it's also the case that we have not one Nobel laureate on our faculty. We have fewer than two dozen members of the National Academy of Sciences. We had a MacArthur ("Genius") award winner, but he left for a more prestigious school soon after arriving, citing Duke's rampant—and institutional—racism. The only other MacArthur Fellow I know of was denied tenure. What we have are a lot of very competent—and a handful of excellent—academics. But seventeen-year-olds aren't that interested in the markers of professional academic achievement, and most of their parents don't know enough to ask. I say we have a great faculty; they take me at my word.

I tell them that you have until the end of your sophomore year to declare your major. You can major in anything you like, from A to Z, from anthropology to zoology. If you can't find something that interests you, then you can invent your own major. Program Two allows you to pull together a series of courses, with the aid of an academic adviser, so you can create your own course of study. We also have minors, and certificate programs, which are like interdisciplinary minors. They're in subjects like primatology, or dance, or Judaic studies. Since so many of our marketing materials feature the Duke Chapel, I try to throw in a bone, every now and then, to the many non-Christians in the audience.

The chapel is the architectural centerpiece of the school; all of the graduate and professional schools are within a five-minute walk of it. I note that the west campus of Duke was designed by an African American architect, Julian Abel, who, in the segregated south of the 1920s, never visited his creation. I point out how far the New South has come.

I talk briefly about the School of Engineering. I tell them that we have a relatively high percentage of women in our engineering school (but still, only about a quarter of the students are women, and from what I've heard from them, it's not an easy road). I tell them that if you're in the School of Engineering, you can double major in Trinity College. I mention my friend Neil. He majored in biomedical engineering, chemistry, and economics. He had two scholarly papers published while an undergrad and has applied for a patent. He played club water polo and taught CPR to third graders. He's also, I say, a hottie. Just a typical engineer, I say.

Yeah, right.

I tell them that they can study abroad, that more than 40 percent of our students choose to study away at some point. For some reason, we feel that this is a powerful and positive statistic. I'm not so sure that it's a good thing. Of course, travel broadens. We all know that. But it seems faintly ironic that students are so anxious to leave—even for a semester—a school they claim to love. I don't bring this up, but instead tell them about Duke in Madrid, Duke in Paris, Duke in Vienna, the newest Duke in—in Havana. (The more astute in the audience murmur.) I tell them about Sarah, a friend who was premed and then went to spend a year studying in northern India, Nepal, and Tibet. When she returned she formed a Duke chapter of Students for a Free Tibet, decided to bag medical school, and wants now to go into the Peace Corps. You're at risk of having a life-changing experience if you go abroad, I tell them.

I give them the statistics about the preprofessional students— the high percentage of admittance to medical, law, and business schools among our students. Of course what I don't tell them is that if a student is not competitive, the premed dean, a wonderful and smart woman, will discourage them from applying. She tells it like it is. Many of them hate her for it.

"Okay," I say, "I'll tell you a little about student life, but I'd rather you hear it directly from a real live student. So I'll just give you my impression of student life at Duke. I can sum it up in one word: tense. It's a high-powered pressure cooker of a place. Students are in the library eighteen hours a day, they never go outside, they never have any fun."

I pause. There's silence, and then a little bit of giggling. "Do you believe me?" They laugh. "Okay, I say, here's the reason I think of *tents*. When I first moved to Durham, I was driving past the gymnasium. I looked out and saw a sea of tents (now they're nodding, getting the homonym) pitched in front of the gym. What's going on, I said? Is there a housing crisis here? People are paying thirty thousand dollars a year to live in tents?

"Well, people do in fact live in tents. Here's the deal. All Duke students get in free—with their thirty thousand dollars a year—to all Duke basketball games. We have not one, but two, excellent teams. Both our men and our women are extremely good. Cameron Indoor Stadium is a really cool place to see basketball games. Part of what makes it so cool is that it's such a small, intimate venue. So everyone wants to go, but not everyone can get a seat. So students line up in advance for tickets. They line up two weeks in advance. What they do is pitch tents—before a Duke-UNC game there will be two hundred tents pitched, with an average of fifteen students per tent. They place numbers on the outside of the tent to signify the place in line. Not all students have to be in the tent at the same time—except the night before the game, when the coach sends out pizza for everyone who's been camping out—but there must be a student in the tent at all times [when classes aren't in session, I add, for the benefit of the parents] to hold the place. It's very organized: Duke student government comes by and does 'tent checks.'

"I decided one day, while coming back from a run, that I would jog around Krzyzewskiville to see what they were doing in these tents. Pause. They were e-mailing. They had an infrared Internet hookup, and they were sitting in their tents, laptops on their laps, e-mailing their mothers. They were doing pharmacokinetic modeling. They were making papier-mâché piñatas. They were writing term papers on Wallace Stevens, and they were having a great time.

"This," I say, "is what you get when you come to Duke." (To my surprise, every time I deliver this corny sentence, I get chills.)

"You get to have it both ways: you get to be at a place where the academics are on a par with every university in the country. You also get to be at a place where the students have fun. And where they love their school. School spirit comes out big-time around basketball, but it also comes out in the support shown for the other twenty-five varsity sports. All of our teams are very good," I say, "except for football. [I pause.] They stink. Last year they managed to 'earn' the record for being the losingest team ever in the league. But, they're really smart guys. Lots of National Merit Scholars on the football team."

This is not true. I say it, anyway, to get a laugh and because that's what these folks want to believe. I pull out the statistic that Duke has the highest graduation rate in Division I football to bolster my outrageous statement. That part, at least, is true.

I go on to tell them that not only are sports a big deal, but so is community service and the arts. I give them examples of things that students are doing (things that all of our peer institutions could easily list as well). But I say them with enthusiasm and affection.

I finish up my spiel, do the admissions portion (which is identical to what I've already told some of these kids when I visited their schools), and open it up to questions. There are the usuals.

General questions about financial aid, specific questions about courses to take, median SAT scores.

In the back of the room a woman stands up.

"I'd just like to add one thing to Rachel's presentation," she says.

"My son is applying to Duke this year because his sister is there. She has had the best three years of her life there and couldn't be happier. We love Duke. If you have any questions, please feel free to come up and talk to me. I love to talk about Duke."

It was an unplanned, unanticipated moment. But it was sincere and warm. I hoped the son was going to be a strong applicant, though I knew that if he was anywhere close to his sister in terms of application criteria, we'd probably admit him. We don't like to deny siblings.

The usual mob scene ensues. I stand around, as if in a receiving line, while parents and applicants come forward to shake my hand. Some have specific questions, most just want to introduce themselves. When it comes time to read applications, I will not remember meeting most of these kids.

Having wrapped up my Massachusetts travel, gotten a good dose of the beauty of a New England fall, and an even bigger shot of the institutional self-satisfaction of Northeastern prep schools, I'm happy to be home, if only briefly. I take my grown-up clothes in to be dry-cleaned (Duke pays for cleaning only if you are on the road longer than two weeks—most of the trips that we take are no more than a week and a half). I pay bills, return phone calls, and sleep happily in my own bed.

Then I hit the road again, this time for my trip to northern California. The office has divided the state between two admissions officers. I get everything north of Bakersfield. I've planned the trip to spend a day in San Francisco, a day in Marin, and one in the East Bay. Then I'll pop down to the "peninsula" and do two days of school visits in the affluent areas around Silicon Valley.

You can't fly direct from Raleigh-Durham to San Francisco, so it's an all-day affair getting out there. Driving into the city from the airport I am struck by the astonishing differences in geography. This is why I wanted this region, I tell myself, because when I am out here I am constantly and geographically blissed out.

But it turns out there's another advantage to recruiting in northern California. Unlike the New England prep school kids, these people are, in general, a bit more laid back. I get fewer questions about early decision, fewer white-knuckled anxiety-ridden applicants and parents wanting to know about the chances for admission. Instead they tend to ask about diversity on campus and whether they can get a good latte.

It takes me a while, though, to form this impression. My first school visit is to the Collegiate School, a private school in the city, which turns out to be all too familiar. The kids are bit hipper than my Boston hopefuls, but the counselor is an imperious Swiss woman who tells me how exceptional her students are. It isn't until I get to the other schools, some of the public magnet schools, that I realize how different these Californians are.

Even superficially, the contrast is striking. Their dress is more relaxed, literally, than my Northeasterners in their pressed khakis and tight-fitting black slacks. Looking out into their faces I see a spectrum of colors: Asians, Latinos, African Americans. And I see, too, an easy interaction between these groups.

Another noticeable difference is their view of Duke. They mention it in the same breath as Harvard, Princeton, and Yale. They don't seem to have the Ivy bias of the New Englanders. It's all on the other side of the country to them, far away and foreign, and for many of them, that is what appeals. They seem less hung up on the name branding of universities, more interested in the culture of the places to which they intend to apply.

I visit a handful of private schools that are similar to those in New England. Ross Academy, nestled in the deep-pocketed county of Marin, drips with the casualness of California money. The counselor, Roger, is an easygoing African American man who had previously been in admissions at an elite Northeastern school and is a straight shooter. I like him immediately. He tells me which of the kids who are applying are likely to receive big pushes from our development office. We manage to take, each year, a number of the weakest applicants from this school because they have such a strong "institutional" push behind them. He knows the score: Ross Academy's admissions standards are also influenced by its development office.

At some public schools there are no guidance counselors at all. Budget cuts have made it necessary for schools to cut back on teachers; college counselors are a luxury. Many of these high schools have "career centers," staffed by parent volunteers. Many of these parents have children who are in the process of applying to college; they listen more intently to my spiel than do the kids. They are not shy about asking questions. The centers have collections of college catalogs, view books, and videos. As I arrive they give me "my file" and ask me to add updated materials, pulling the things that are no longer relevant. In this way I get to see what Duke's marketing campaign looked like, going back a number of years.

At some schools I see big roomfuls of kids, all of whom are interested in Duke and fairly well informed. At others, there are one or two students, meeting with me in order to get out of class. I can tell within a few questions that they are probably not going to be competitive applicants. But, as a good recruiter, I do nothing to discourage their applications.

"Your SATs are below our median? That shouldn't stop you. You just don't know what we might find appealing about you when you send in your application." We want them to send in their applications, not only so that we will have greater numbers and a lower rate of admittance, but also so that we will have their sixty-dollar application fee.

I am invited to a "college night" at a good private school in a pastoral setting. There is to be first a panel discussion, and then each of the invited college reps (there are eight of us) will have our own table from which we can talk to interested kids and parents. This night is only for this one school; they have not invited students from public schools in the surrounding area. Their senior class is small—only about a hundred kids. This is the kind of personalized attention you get when you pay tuition that almost equals what it costs to go to college.

An interesting collection of schools is represented here. Some large public universities, some small liberal arts colleges, representing a range of selectivity. What strikes me most is how alike we sound when we describe our schools. We all boast small-college seminar experience in the context of a larger academic setting. We all have faculty who are committed first and foremost to teaching undergraduates but who are also world-renowned scholars; we all have great athletic teams, and our athletes are all academic superstars. We all have Internet access in dorm rooms for our students, and the food at each school is delicious, varied, and healthy.

When we talk about admissions, we all mention the same things. Each question is addressed by the panelists in turn, from right to left. The people on the left side do a lot of "as my colleagues have already said" answering. There are a few gray-haired wizened old pros, but most of the admissions professionals are tidy young women in suits, who speak clearly and confidently and end up looking and sounding like flight attendants.

I had planned two Duke nights during my California trip. One was to be held on the peninsula for the applicants from the affluent areas around Palo Alto. I chose a hotel just across the street from Stanford as my venue. For the one in the Bay Area, I'd been advised that doing it in San Francisco proper would be a nightmare because of transportation and parking. Since I had family in Berkeley, had spent a good amount of time there, and liked it (how can you not like a city with so many good bookstores and restaurants?), I decided to use a hotel in Berkeley, right off the freeway. I figured that it would be easy both for the people coming from Marin County and for those coming through the tunnel from Contra Costa County. I was not prepared for the reaction that met this decision. People actually seemed afraid to come to Berkeley.

The Duke night was therefore not nearly as well attended as the one I'd hold later in swanky Palo Alto. But I liked the people more. After my presentation a tall willowy blonde—the epitome of the California girl—comes up to me.

She introduces herself as Amelia.

"Look," she says, "I've been raised in the Bay Area my whole life. I'm an ecofeminist and I do workshops on facilitating interactions between children of different races. I baby-sit for kids who only speak Spanish, and I tutor a Cambodian girl. I'm worried that Duke will be a little too homogenous for me. What do you think?"

What could I say? This was just the kind of kid I wanted at Duke. Of course I knew nothing about her academic achievement, but in terms of her extracurricular interests, she was my cup of tea. With more kids like this it would be possible, I thought, to change or at least to affect the dominant culture at the school. But would she be happy? Would she find it oppressively politically apathetic? Would she be able to find a cohort of like-minded friends, and would she be able to open the minds of the Southern frat boys?

"Here's what you should do," I tell her. "Visit the campus, if you can. I'll arrange for you to stay in a dorm room with a current Duke student. That way you can see for yourself if you think you'll feel comfortable."

Not a good answer, because it assumes she has the resources to take that kind of a trip. But what else could I say?

She nods and thanks me.

Next a well-dressed, well-groomed woman who I assumed had to be in her forties but looked younger than I came up with her son.

"Hi, Rachel. Susan Brandon. I've heard about you from Roger."

Roger was the counselor at Ross Academy, the private school in Marin I'd visited two days before.

"This is my son, Justin."

Justin was a handsome, well-built guy.

"Justin plays football at Ross. He's the starting quarterback. It's an incredible time commitment."

"I see," I say, though I don't.

"We've been talking with the development office at Duke. But I understand that you are the person who will be reading Justin's application, so I wanted to make sure you had a chance to meet him personally."

Now I am beginning to see. I would bet he didn't break 1300 on his SATs, and his transcript was, er, less than stellar.

A tall, skinny lanky girl comes up and asks about North Carolina residency. "I'm Shawn, from Zebulon, North Carolina," she says, "but I'm finishing up high school here in Oakland."

"Home of the Mudcats!" I say, referring to the town's minor league baseball team. "You like it out here?"

"Yeah, well it's a kind of complicated situation."

"Okay," I say, "just make sure that you explain it on your application."

"Here's my question: Do I count as a North Carolinian or a Californian?"

"What's your home address?" I ask. She tells me that officially she still lives with her mother, in Raleigh.

"You're in luck. While I'll be the one reading your application, you will get the extra considerations we give to North Carolinians. Our only quota is to keep thirteen percent of the class from North Carolina."

What I don't say to her is that this means that the standards for admitting North Carolinians are much, much lower. What I used to say behind closed doors is that basically, if you're a North Carolinian and breathe, you get in. The North Carolina admissions officer rightly took issue with my sniping comments and defended her kids against my cheap shots.

"Great, great," she says. "I enjoyed your presentation. I grew up going over to Duke for various things, but I never really saw it before. You made me excited about applying. In fact, I'm going to apply early decision."

"Wonderful. Tell me your name?"

"Shawn. Shawn White."

"Great, Shawn. I'll keep an eye out for your application."

A couple dozen more hands to shake, and then I head back to my aunt and uncle's place, exhausted.

I write up my notes on the school visits—how many kids I saw at each school, how many were juniors, how many seniors, comments, when appropriate, on my interactions with the counselor, or noting if there was no counselor. I write notes on the Berkeley Duke night. I'm not sure that someone else would have chosen to have a Duke night in Berkeley. It's not easy to answer questions from the audience about the number of African Americans on the faculty (especially since most of them are in the medical center); it's not easy to answer questions about the political climate at Duke, about the engagement of the student body with activist issues. These people don't want to hear about basketball and sunny weather. I like these people; but most likely the best applicants among them will be admitted to Duke and will choose not to attend.

The Duke night in Palo Alto is a different story. I've never seen so many healthy-and wealthy-looking people gathered together in one place. The questions were less edgy, more focused on getting in, security issues on campus, and if freshman were allowed to have cars.

Scads of alumni also showed up for my presentation. These people were diehards; they expressed disappointment that someone in my job had not gone to Duke. They criticized my portrayal of the climate as no longer "work hard, play hard." I chose to talk about the students I knew: the ones who were involved in more intellectual pursuits (like applying for patents) and more activist causes, like my friend who had started Students Against Sweatshops. They wanted me to talk about basketball and fraternities. They did not like me, these peninsular alums.

In general the Duke alumni I met were pleasant enough, but clearly they were the bright, well-rounded (and well-heeled) types that make up the Duke stereotype. I can't help but think how much easier it was to get into Duke when they applied. While traveling I heard more from middle-aged people about their own college experiences than I ever thought I would. Their homes are decked out with Duke paraphernalia. They give up evenings and afternoons to attend college fairs on behalf of Duke; they wear the school colors by showing up at my Duke nights and helping to turn on and off the lights for the slide show. And they talk about their experiences as Duke students as if it were only yesterday that they were haunting the campus instead twenty or thirty years ago.

I have perhaps been on the road too long. I am tired of living out of a suitcase, wearing the same clothes, and saying the same things day after day. When I'm asked a question, almost invariably one I've been asked the day—or even the hour—before, I go on autopilot and spill out my canned response. My mouth moves, my brain remains still. This is not a good way to recruit.

I have an extra day and night in California, and go back up to Marin County to see Scott, a man I'd met the summer before. He lives in paradise. And he has a horse, a big chestnut Arabian named Mouse, with whom I'd fallen hopelessly in love. We go for a twenty-mile trail ride through the scrubby hills of Marin, and later that night Scott cooks me a dinner of fried abalone and pours me a few good glasses of Alexander Valley chardonnay. I am restored.

This is why, I remember, I wanted to recruit in northern California.

4

A Mind of Winter: *Learning to Read*

A pig is not a dog. Or a cat. Or a horse. Species matters. What you think you know about animals just doesn't translate in the porcine world.

Emma, a three-year-old Vietnamese pot-bellied pig, is a force of nature. She insists on sleeping not only on the bed, but between the sheets. I coparent her with my ex-boyfriend Andrew. We got her a number of years after we'd broken up, and have had our biggest arguments about proper pig parenting. We got her partly because pigs are hypoallergenic. Andrew loved my dog, Hannah; he loved less having to embark on a weekly series of allergy shots. When we broke up, he missed Hannah and wanted to get a pet of his own. I suggested that he consider a pig. They don't lick themselves and they only shed once a year.

Neither of us was quite prepared for Emma. She can open doors, cabinets, childproof medicine bottles, zippers, bags, snaps, clips, and purses. Nothing is sacred, nothing is safe, and nothing seems to slow her down. She is a forty-seven-pound dynamo built like a linebacker, with twice the intelligence and a thousand times the persistence.

One of the main differences in having a pig as a companion animal comes from the fact that much of the world eats your pet. I can't tell you how many times, while we're trotting down the street, someone comments on lunch, dinner, or barbecue. Although there are cultures that do eat dogs and cats, there's nothing like taking a walk with an incipient pork chop to get you thinking about vegetarianism.

While dogs will occasionally happen upon something to eat while outdoors, for a pig, a walk in the park is like traveling through a delicious salad bowl. Clover is a particular favorite, but other, more carefully tended flowers are also appealing. Acorn season is a nightmare when trying to walk a pig.

Emma is a consumer. She'll eat anything—except for onions, parsley, and celery. She once ate a box of green tea, including the bags, and was then so caffeinated that she bucked like a bronco and couldn't settle down for an entire night. She can and does drink copious amounts of water. We have marveled many times about the capacity, the apparent elasticity, of her bladder. Andrew has timed her pees. He's clocked her at up to three minutes. No kidding.

Emma has many different and distinct vocalizations. She moos. She growls. She has a special feed-me noise that is like a combination duck-bullfrog. If she can't get a response from me, she will often approach Hannah, her canine elder sibling, and ask her for food. When bored, Emma oinks incessantly and wags her tail. When thinking, she's eerily still and silent. Silence from the pig is often cause for alarm.

Emma has no moral center. Like a dog, she knows when she's bad. Unlike a dog, she doesn't care.

It's not easy to love a pig, but I just can't help loving Emma. Perhaps that's because she's bonded to me. Or perhaps there's something about me, and the Pig Daddy, that makes us doting pig parents. I love the devoted enthusiasm of dogs. I appreciate the arrogant self-possession of cats. But I am drawn to the challenge, the oddity, of sharing my life with a pig. She is a hoofed reminder of the inscrutability of the other, an oinking instantiation of the idea that difference makes a difference. Species—like race, like gender—matters.

After weeks on the road, spending time at home with my dog and my pig feels like a vacation. November gets taken up with early decision. It's a dress rehearsal for the reading and selection committee meetings we will have later.

During my recruiting travel I heard many kids say, "I know I'm going to apply early; I just don't know where." This is a sentence that makes admissions folk cringe. Early decision programs, where a student selects her first choice school and agrees, if admitted, to matriculate, were designed for students who had truly been able to make their college decision early; they had found their perfect match and knew that they wanted to look no further. It was a way for the applicant to say to the school, "I want you," and for the school to admit those kids who would turn into die-hard alumni.

Early decision programs were not meant to be used as an admissions strategy, but instead they were a compassionate way to ease anxiety and allow students to enjoy (think of it!) their senior year in high school, knowing that they had a place in a class they were truly enthusiastic about joining. That's a great sentiment. I'm not sure how much truth there is to it these days.

Duke's program is early decision. This means that if we admit a kid, they are contractually obligated to come, unless the financial aid package is not going to be sufficient. It's usually not a problem. (A large percentage of the early kids do not apply for aid.) There are schools that have early action programs, wherein they notify kids that they have been admitted but do not demand that they commit. We could never afford to do that; too many of our top admits turn us down ultimately for "better" schools.

For admissions officers it's a relaxed, leisurely introduction to the whole process. The applicant pool is smaller by an order of magnitude: I had just over one hundred applicants. I got to admit eighteen; eleven were admitted with special-interest codes; fifteen were denied, and the rest were deferred. Of those deferred, we expected to admit maybe one or two in regular decision rounds. Maybe none.

The early decision process is different also because these are the kids who tell you they are dying for Duke. They have their heart set on the school, and they are hell-bent on getting in. I have been receiving e-mails from a lot of these kids, giving me updates on their activities and achievements, sometimes just checking in to say hello. We don't reject many of them outright, thinking it's gentler to defer them (even if we know that we will not admit them in April). This means that they get another four months to plead their cases. Some—the ones who are most persistent and annoying through early December— I argue to have denied, rather than deferred, so that I will not have to endure more months of pestering.

One of my favorite kids was Domenic Berardi, from Adams High School, just north of Boston. He was the valedictorian of his class, first out of 179; he had taken eight APs, and his record of straight As was unblemished. His guidance counselor called him "The most insightful young man ever. Dream child." His English teacher wrote that he "excels as a writer; one of most talented and likable ever in twenty-seven years of teaching." His American government teacher concurred: "One of the most remarkable in twenty-one years—don't let this one get away." It was a three-and-a-half page recommendation, describing in detail how Dom had, on his own, read all of the Federalist papers and most of the Anti-Federalist papers.

His book essay was about Jake Brigance, the hero of John Grisham's not very good novel A *Time to Kill*. He talked about the love of family, having a strong work ethic, and the importance of racial tolerance. His long essay was quite remarkable. It began, "Hey Dom, would you give a hand putting this body into the casket?" It was about his summer job the past three years, working in a funeral home. It was a striking meditation on the complexity of grief, on learning about bodies and mortality, and on his growing interest in the field of medicine. His E-mail address was "Doogie."

He was class president junior and senior year; president of Peer Mediation; played soccer, tennis, and piano, was an announcer at school football and basketball games, and was heavily involved in local politics.

I loved this kid. I looked at the information on his parents. He was first-generation college! His dad was an electrician, his mom a secretary. He was in.

As were my guys from the Eliot School. The little one, Jon, turned out to be a strong applicant, having hosted his own TV show, run three marathons, and demonstrated a keen interest in Soviet culture. Since we usually didn't get exciting kids early decision, we took him. His buddy, Brent, like most of the rest of the early kids, was a child of privilege.

Early decision privileges the already privileged. A high school student who has a college counselor or parents who are able to push them to start thinking about college in their junior year, who realizes early on that it's important to be thoughtful about applying to college, who can afford to spend the summer traveling around and visiting schools, interviewing, comparing, and then have their applications ready to go by the fall is going to have a big leg up in this business.

Since the reading load for early decision was so light, it was easy to spend time lingering languidly over their applications, searching for reasons to have them admitted, to get to know them well. During rounds we would be admonished repeatedly to bear in mind the regret factor: we knew that each year the early pool was much, much weaker than the regular pool. Kids that looked great to us in November would pale in comparison to the applications we'd be reading in January. They were generally the BWRKs, and early decision was the only time we would take them. Most of them were not particularly interesting, but after all of that time traveling, when you finally sat down to read their applications you couldn't help but love them.

After they were admitted, they would continue to e-mail

throughout the year. They may not have been the strongest applicants, but they sure were eager.

The turnaround for early decision is quick. The deadline is November first, and we go into selection committee before Thanksgiving. The first couple of weeks in December we spend getting the decisions out and then dealing with the aftermath.

After the first of the year the time-pressured period for students, when they must scurry to finish their essays, to complete their applications, is over. Many of them have pulled all-nighters to get their stuff in the mail to us. That haste will show in the applications and will not work in their favor. For most, now, all they can do is wait until April. Fat envelope or thin. There's a lot of time to worry, but nothing more can be done. This is when our real work begins. From now until when the letters are stuffed, we will kick into high gear: reading, selecting, arguing in committee, and processing the decisions.

For the first two weeks of January we open mail. Both "professional" and operations staff work two shifts to open all the mail that comes in just before the January second deadline. I volunteer, with Audrey, Victoria, and Chuck, to be on the night shift. This means we don't have to come in until 2:00 P.M. and we stay until 10:00 each night. We bring in music and food, and we don't have to wear dress-up clothes. I bring in my dog, Hannah, and Emma, the pig. We like working the night shift.

We open priority mail and FedEx packets. We open letters containing teacher recommendations. We sort them into piles, by parts of the applications. Checks and part I are important, as they must be entered first into the computer. Transcripts and teacher recommendations go together, and the personal portion, part 5, is sorted into regular testers and high testers—those who have scored above 1480.

We also open boxes of wacky stuff. "Here's a shoe," I read, from a note accompanying a worn-out running shoe. "I just want to get my foot in the door." Another kid sends in his trusty old Duke hat. Pinned to it is a note: "I'll pick this up when I get to campus in August." "I don't think so," says Chuck, pitching it into one of the buckets of stuff to be placed in applicants' files.

"Here's one of yours," Audrey calls out to me. "Must be the editor of the paper at Jonathan Edwards School." There's a thick sheaf of newspapers included with the part 5 of the application.

"Turkish Delight," I say, opening a big box. "We know who this is for." As the person who reads the international applications, each year Audrey gets loads of Turkish Delight from our many Turkish applicants. (There is no financial aid available at Duke for international students.)

I open a priority-mail envelope and a cassette tape falls out. The label reads, "Me speaking French."

We open. We sort.

"Wow, check this out," says Chuck. "A girl with a 1550 and she's written her essay on running. She also, according to her extracurricular sheet, started a feminist poetry club and she rides horses. Sounds like one for you, Rachel."

"Bad poetry, no doubt," I say. "Let me see that running essay."

He hands it over and I start to read. It's good, very good.

"I hope that bozo realizes that this is a good essay when he reads it," I say.

"You just calm down now," Chuck says to me. "Or I'm not going to show you this other kid I just found—one of yours, with a letter of recommendation from a *Very* Famous Person."

After two weeks, we are released from our manual labor. We are expected to be in the office two half days a week. All of us come in on Tuesday mornings for the weekly staff meeting, and one other half day. The rest of the time we spend at home, reading.

I'll just read five more, then I'll let myself go downstairs and get a cup of tea. It's cold in here. Maybe I should get a sweater. No, I'll read these five and then take a break.

The payoff after all that travel is that now I have bucketloads of applications to read. Though the high testers are supposed to be read first, the vagaries of the filing system make this difficult. So I have a mixed bag, of high testers and the eager beavers who sent in their apps months before the deadline and then pestered their teachers to make sure the applications were complete.

I am living amid pink and blue folders. Not for girls and boys, but for arts and sciences and engineering. At Duke, as at many schools, applicants must apply to individual schools. All they do is check a separate box. But we look at them a little differently. The engineers must look like engineers to be admitted. That means they have to have strong testing, especially in math. And they must have taken the hardest math and science courses available to them. There is a completely different formula for computing their reader rating sums, an equation invented by the engineering faculty so that we would admit the kind of future engineers that they were looking for. These people believe in standardized testing.

I've got myself into a nice routine. I wake early, usually around six. Go downstairs, feed the dog and the pig, have breakfast and peruse, in a leisurely way, the paper. Then, still before seven, I go upstairs to my study to read. I read in my pajamas, lilac flannel with little penguins on them and the words *pole nord*. I usually work until at least eleven, when I put on my running clothes and go for a run. I come home, shower, get dressed, and read for another few hours. I'll eat dinner, sometimes with friends, and then resume reading until around ten.

The hard part is the monotony, trying to make sure that you are fresh enough to give each kid a fair read. We read to say yes, rather than no. Looking for some reason to admit the kid. Most of the time we don't find one.

All of the applications are read initially by a team of first readers. A lot of what they do is clerical: they begin the process of filling out the reader-rating form. They fill in the applicant's name (first, last, and preferred) and file number. They circle whether the applicant is male or female, applying to arts and sciences or engineering. They write in the name of the high school, its zip code and ETS code.

Then there are a bunch of other blanks. They fill in such items as "language spoken at home." It's important to know for an Asian kid, say, who may have stellar math testing and grades but is weaker on the verbal side, if his family doesn't speak English at home. They note if the applicant has disclosed special needs, for example, a physical or learning disability. We are, under the Americans with Disabilities Act, not allowed to treat these scores any differently. If a student has been professionally diagnosed with a learning disability, we cannot take that into account in our deliberations. Unfortunately, many students with disabilities are being counseled by their college counselors not to disclose them and are told not to opt for the nonstandard (either untimed or in a distraction-free environment) administration of the tests. There's a reason for this advice. Many schools do look askance at nonstandard admissions of tests. Recent studies have shown that the vast majority of them are administered to white males from high-income families.

The reader-rating card has a place to record the academic interest of the applicant, though at Duke this information is really not used. Other schools do use it—and measure premeds against other premeds, the cutthroat competition beginning before they ever walk into an organic chemistry lecture. Or if a student applies to a school's fine arts division and has shown no interest in the arts, they might be torpedoed. Or if they want fashion design, and the school doesn't offer it, small liberal arts colleges may take this as an indication of lack of strong interest in attending and not give the student an opportunity to turn down the school. One private university in the Boston area is known for not admitting its best-qualified students; they're trying to shake the reputation of being a safety school.

Special talents in art, music, dance, or theater are noted, as are special factors. These could include whether or not there's a parent or sibling tie to the school, or if, on the other hand, the applicant is first-generation college. No admissions committee can resist a good first-gen college kid. One of the most important blanks to be filled out is relationships. First readers are warned never to overlook this category and to make sure that they note the name, year of graduation, and degree of parents or siblings who attended Duke. Siblings will be looked up in the "bible," the set of historical printouts of reader ratings, and the admissions officer will record their information. Generally applicants who are as good as or better than their older siblings are admitted. And even parents who never stayed for a degree—house-staff doctors or people who did a one-year fellowship— are counted in the relationship category.

Standardized test scores and the dates they were taken are all recorded. SATI/SAT II, ACT, TOEFL. If test scores are reported by the student and not verified either by the transcript from the ETS or the school transcript, the scores are circled as "self-reported," the circles reminding us that they are not official and may not be, um, accurate.

GPA, both weighted and unweighted, and rank in class, again, weighted or not, are noted, as is the percentage of college-bound students from the high school. This figure is extremely helpful in understanding a school that may not send very many applicants. A kid who's maxed out the curriculum at a school that offers only two AP courses where only 25 percent of the students go on to four-year schools may be expected to have lower board scores.

The senior class schedule is recorded. Senior year is when most students take their hardest load. We get grades for the first quarter by early decision, and by midterm for regular decision. We look at these senior-year grades. Often a straight-A student will get her first C in calculus senior year. Students will also often take courses at local colleges during their senior year, especially if they've exhausted the curriculum at their high school. So on the reader-rating card there will be a list of senior-year courses: AP calculus BC, AP biology, AP European history, Spanish 4, Honors English. First readers note the number of advanced-placement courses offered at the school and the total number taken by the applicant.

The first readers go over the transcript and record every grade received starting in ninth grade. They fill in what is called the "grade grid." You have to be prepared, in committee, to "give the grid." It sounds something like "Five and one; four and two; six and zero; two, three, and one." That corresponds to the number of As, Bs, and Cs each year. You must do it in that order, you must place the "ands" in the correct place so that the committee can easily follow it, or else risk the wrath of the director. A GPA of 3.8, say, can look very different for different students. It can be a mix of As and Bs, or it can be all As with one particularly bad year or semester. A student may have faltered at the beginning of their high school career and started out with more Bs than As, then worked up to straight As. So it's important, while reading and especially while making a case to selection committee, to be able to note what the grade trend has been.

The first readers sift through the transcript and report only the grades for what we call academic "solids": math, science, social science, English, and foreign language. Courses in religion and computer science are noted but not counted. Courses in studio art, music, accounting, gym, debate, shop, journalism, yearbook are not included in the academic load, though AP courses in arts and computer science do count. The first readers also note how many solids have been taken each year, and of those, how many are honors level and how many are Advanced Placement.

The first readers assign three reader ratings: curriculum choice, achievement, and recommendations. The scale is one to five, with five being the highest. There are further ratings used by admissions officers for essays and personal qualities/extracurriculars. A reader-rating card will have two columns of numbers, one from the first reader (but only for the first three ratings) and the other for the five ratings from the officer. A sixth rating is added, by the computer, for testing.

In order to be a competitive applicant at Duke, most students will need to have fives in the first two ratings and a five in testing (1480 and above). To get a five in curriculum choice the applicant must show evidence of having taken the most rigorous program available in a competitive high school. That means that they must have taken at least five solids for each year of high school and have taken at least five AP courses. Duke, along with other schools, has become a slave to that moneymaking enterprise, the College Board. Because it's widespread, and because it's an easy—though perhaps not wholly accurate—way to measure rigor, many schools simply count AP courses to determine how strong an applicant's curriculum is. This can encourage coaching toward the test rather than teaching, or thinking. A number of the better private schools don't label their courses as AP but say instead that they prepare students for the tests.

Although the scores on the tests were meant, originally, for placement into higher level college courses and were not intended to be used in college admissions, they are. We expect students to score fives on their tests. If they get a couple of fours, that's OK, but anything below a four doesn't help much. We don't require that students report these scores for admission; if they do, however, we use them. I always told students that if they scored below a four, not to report it to us. But many schools place the test scores on the transcripts. The International Baccalaureate curriculum is becoming more common, and any student taking the full IB diploma will automatically receive a five in curriculum choice.

For those applicants whose schools don't offer the opportunity to take five AP courses the best curriculum rating they can be assigned is a four. But the four is circled on the reader-rating card to signify that it's the best available. Students will also get a four if they take only three or four AP courses. Honors-level courses are expected and therefore not given much special significance.

If a student is at a good public high school, say in suburban Boston, and has not stretched herself by taking hard courses, she is not likely to get into a school like Duke.

For many of the private schools, figuring out the strength of curriculum is more complicated. You can't just count AP courses. Almost all schools will send along a school profile, giving general information about the school as well as a listing of the more advanced classes. The elite private schools send along a course catalog. In order to understand what a student is taking, you have to get to know the school and the individual courses. Sometimes you even have to understand the differences between teachers. That's why we read regionally.

The second rating is for academic achievement. It's separated from curriculum choice so that students who want to take easy courses in order to bolster their GPAs can do that, but it won't help them get into a school like Duke. In order to get a five in achievement the applicant must be in the top 1 or 2 percent of their graduating class. In reality, she should be in the top two places, and should have all As. It's hard to get a five in achievement if your transcript is blemished with a B. Kids from elite private schools rarely get fives in achievement. And only the top few from the good pubic schools do. Mostly the fives go to the valedictorians. More and more schools are deciding not to rank their students. It fosters an atmosphere of competitiveness, they say. Many of the private schools gave up ranking a long time ago. Why should parents pay twenty thousand dollars or thirty thousand dollars to send their kid to a school where he will be in the middle of the class when, if they kept him in a local public school, he'd rise like cream to the top? Prep schools were meant to prepare kids for college, and the counselors at these schools have their headmasters and boards of trustees to answer to if their kids don't get in. Obfuscation of rank in class has become something of an art.

In order to get a four in achievement, a student must be in the top decile of the class at a very competitive school or the top 5 percent at a less competitive one. Generally they are A students that have a few Bs.

The last rating that the first readers assign is for recommendations. Ratings in this area are a combination of the letters from the counselor and teachers, and the check marks on our form that we ask them to fill in. If a teacher checks a five, it should mean that this student is one of the top few they have encountered in their teaching career. There's space on the reader-rating card for C (counselor), T1 (teacher one), and T2 (teacher two). If the applicant has had an interview, and it has been written up, there is a space for the "Int" rating. There are three required recommendations, one from the counselor, two from teachers. We tell the kids that they must have two teacher recs, from junior or senior year, and they must be from people who have taught them in academic solids. In reality, we consider an application complete even if there's only one teacher rec. Naturally, it's better to have two, but only rarely are they significantly different, and, more important, we are usually so pinched for time that we can't afford to wait for both to be received in order to make our evaluations. We don't tell kids this.

The counselors fill out a form that gives some general information about the school: number of students in the graduating class, number of AP courses offered, percentage to four year colleges and universities, and then information about the specific applicant. Many of the counselors in big public high schools are writing their recommendations without much personal knowledge of the student. We ask them what their counseling load is and what other responsibilities they have in their jobs. Even when they write from school records only they are still able to tell us about any disciplinary actions that may have been taken against the student and any other special circumstances of note. Often they will let us know if something happened that affected a large number of student in the class, say the death of a classmate or a fire in the school.

At smaller schools, and at most of the privates, the counselors tend to know the students very well indeed, either from lengthy counseling sessions or from teaching them in class. A good counselor—and there are some good counselors—will be able to tell an admissions officer helpful and insightful things about each student who's applying and what sets them apart from the others.

The counselor's job at these schools is to get their kids into the best colleges and universities. They are evaluated by how many admits they have to each of the top schools. There is pressure from heads of schools, boards of trustees, and most especially parents. I would not trust many of these people to recommend a good restaurant, let alone give me an honest assessment of an applicant's intellectual abilities. A few years before I entered the business, the college counselor at one of my schools had apparently been lying about the numbers of students admitted to elite colleges. He was found out and, tragically, committed suicide. Most of the people in these jobs take great pains to explain to you how their grades are seriously deflated, how the teacher's expectations are unrelentingly demanding. Sometimes they suppress information that you, as an admissions officer, would both want to know and would hold against a kid, like disciplinary actions taken for violence or cheating. Their job is to get the kids in. I didn't meet many college counselors that I wanted to befriend.

Teacher recommendations run the gamut, from long, writerly meditations to single brief sentences. It's important when reading them not to hold bad teachers against the students. Many teachers simply do not know how to write helpful recommendations. Many have learned what admissions officers are looking for. Usually we're hoping for a single phrase: "My best student in thirty years of teaching." That's a necessary but not sufficient clause to get a five in recs. It's astonishing how many teachers have, each year, the best student they've had in thirty years of teaching. Generally they use the same words and phrases over and over: conscientious, consistent, creative, critical thinker, dedicated, determined, diligent, energetic, enthusiastic, excellent, exceptional, hardworking, honest, independent, insightful, intelligent, learning for learning's sake, mature, motivated, organized, outstanding, perceptive, persistent, positive, problem-solving skills, responsible, scholar, tenacious, well rounded, work ethic.

In the press of reading so many applications in such a short time, admissions officers look for certain words or phrases. The Ds—diligent, disciplined, determined—tend to ring a death knell. We expect that. We expect much more. The best teacher recommendation will tell us what the student is like in the classroom, not on the stage or the football field. They will point to specific examples of intellectual spark and vitality.

The first readers pull out the germane words and phrases from the recs. "Always top of the class—great potential math, rare creative energy—caring" and "high 'A' marks—unbridled enthusiasm." Admissions officers should be astute readers of recommendations, looking for nuances, both of what the letters are saying and what they're not saying. They should be able to recognize the cases in which a student might be better than a school.

Teachers and counselors frequently do applicants a disservice by focusing on character or extracurricular activities and not giving us the academic information we need. If they focus on personal rather than academic qualities, it will hurt the student. In some cases, a teacher will have a student whom she thinks is excellent academically but not a nice person. Those are difficult recommendations to write, and it's important to read them carefully. Many teachers think that the transcript speaks for itself—it never does—and they want to tell us what a sweet person the student is. Many of us have had the experience of reading an identical "personal" letter of recommendation written by a teacher for a number of different students. Usually they remember to use their spell checker to make sure the student's name has been changed in the appropriate places.

We have in our office a recommendation of the year contest, to reward, in a purely honorary way, those teachers who do an outstanding job. We nominate our picks and then send a letter to the winner, and to the head of the winner's school. The best recs aren't always for the best students. The most helpful ones are the most honest, and that may mean that their recommendation is not entirely positive.

Most students waive their right to see the recommendations, though not all do. When they don't waive, we're suspicious. In cases where there may be something amiss with the application, the counselor (sometimes a teacher, though not usually) will add a Post-it note to the letter. While the letter is an official document and goes into the permanent file of the student, the Post-it note doesn't. Sometimes they will just write, "Call me." That's a red flag, and call them we do. What they're willing to say in a telephone call can be far different from what goes into the permanent record. In such a litigious moment, the phone is a better communications device than either letters or E-mail.

To get a five in recommendations a student must be the top of the top. Both teachers and the counselor must convince us that this student is outstanding in every respect. Reading and decoding the recommendations is one of the hardest jobs for an admissions officer. You must read both what is there and what is not there. Just as the grades at the best private schools are deflated, so, too, are the recommendations. Rarely do you see a teacher at one of the top private schools write that a student is "best of career."

Generally the kids we admit are 555 for the first three ratings. Chuck surmised that while we take kids who are 554—kids whose teachers say that they're the best this year, but perhaps not the best ever—these same applicants tend to be wait-listed by Harvard, Princeton, and Yale. He was told that Harvard weights each of its three recommendations individually, so they end up counting for a lot more in the process. This makes a lot of sense. The teacher recommendations are ultimately the best tool for evaluating applications. They are the one part of the process completely out of the control of applicants and their parents. There's not much anyone can do—even the pricey independent college counselors—about how a student responds in the classroom. Even if a student refuses to waive the confidentiality of the recommendation, a good teacher can still tell us more than anyone else—even, and perhaps especially, the applicant—about a kid's intellectual prowess and potential.

You learn a lot about the state of education in the United States by reading thousands of teacher recommendations. There are some good, smart people teaching high school. Sometimes they are as good and as smart as they think they are. The elite private school recommendations often irritated me: the sense of self-importance and solipsism—especially among the older generation—I found annoying. I tried not to hold it against the kids. I was also frequently horrified by letters that could fairly be described as illiterate. And racial stereotyping and prejudice abounded: African American women were often sexualized in their teacher's descriptions—"beautiful," "striking," "elegant," "statuesque," "exotic looks." African American males who were good students were almost invariably referred to as "articulate." Asian kids suffered at the hands of their teachers for not being aggressive enough in classroom discussions, and in the counselor recommendations if they didn't participate in the "life of the school." Sometimes the counselor would mention their commitments at home and to outside jobs; often you'd have to read the complete application to know that these kids worked thirty hours a week in their parents' store or business.

When the first readers are finished with an application, they will have filled out all of the grades and other detailed information, have written highlights from the recommendations in shorthand, and have assigned ratings for curriculum choice, achievement, and recommendations. The admissions officer then gets the folder. She assigns ratings for each of these areas as well. Often, especially in the case of private schools whose curricula are less standard, the rating for curriculum choice will be different. A first reader won't know, for example, that history 30 at one school is equivalent to AP U.S. history. If the admissions officer disagrees, she can send the folder back to the first reader and ask that the rating be changed. Or she can give the higher rating, so the applicant will have a four/five for curriculum choice instead of two fives. Usually the first readers will defer to the officers; sometimes they get territorial, especially those who have been doing it for a while, and want to "discuss." Admissions officers don't have a lot of time to devote to these discussions. I didn't have much patience for them. Ultimately the authority rests with the officer. Some of the first readers pride themselves on being "tough." This isn't particularly helpful, as you want, ideally, to have everyone using the same standards. The first readers, like the admissions officers, read the way they would like to be read.

The admissions officer has space on the right side of the reader-rating card to write her own comments from the recommendations. If the first readers are good, there's not much else to record. Sometimes you'll just place a check mark to note that the first reader has gotten everything important, or you'll note "PQs" to signify that the teacher addresses only personal qualities and not academic strengths.

Although most of the admitted students will have 555 or 554 in their first three reader ratings, it's rare to see a kid from one of the really excellent high schools have such high ratings. Their numbers are generally deflated. This gets taken into account during selection committee.

At the bottom of the reader-rating card are three additional areas for notes by the officer. The extracurriculars are generally a laundry list. Applicants send in pages and pages on what they do, and we distill them back down to a few lines: Glee Club pres, lacrosse; Amnesty International, National Honor Society, though most of us don't even write down NHS, since almost all of our applicants are in it, and it's more unusual not to see it on an application. Same thing for *Who's Who in American High Schools* entries.

A surprising number of our applicants have private pilot's licenses, are certified in scuba, have skied the Alps, sailed the Caribbean, climbed Kilamanjaro, trekked in Nepal, and are active in the National Charity League. These children tend not to apply for financial aid.

There are lots of competitions for science and math students; not all competitions are viewed equally. Taking the American High School Math Exam (AHSME) is not impressive; taking the American Invitational Math Exam (AIME) can be, depending on the score earned. The U.S. Math Olympiad tends to be more selective than the Science and Chemistry Olympiads. Individual competition means more than being part of a team.

Governor's schools are generally competitive and thus are more meaningful than kids taking part in a university summer program, in which participation is often a result of ability to pay. The Bausch and Lomb Science Award is awarded at most schools; college and university Book Awards are given out at many. Boys and Girls State representatives are a dime a dozen; Boys and Girls Nation attendees are fewer and farther between. Among the more meaningless activities (in addition to NHS and *Who's Who*) are Beta Club, Youth in Government, Youth Leadership, Peer Tutor, Peer Counselor, National French/Spanish/Latin exams, Quiz Bowl, Knowledge Bowl, Hugh O'Brien Youth Foundation. I was always personally most turned off by Junior Statesmen of America and by kids who started investment clubs at their schools.

Being an Intel (formerly Westinghouse) finalist, that was impressive. As was attendance at Telluride, a highly selective summer program. Most extracurricular activities, in order to make a difference, had to be accomplished on a national level. That's what you'd need to get a five in PQs/ECs.

It's not unusual to see a student who hasn't done much of anything in the way of extracurricular activities through their first three years of high school start joining lots of clubs in their senior year. Many of our wealthy applicants seem to start clubs to help the needy their senior year. Most kids end up with a three for their PQ/EC rating. A typical list for a typical three might be: Student Council, VP 12; SADD, Treasurer 12; Chess, capt 12; baseball 9, 10; soccer, 11, 12; Outing Club, VP12; church. A busy kid, a good kid. A BWRK. A three. Not impressive in our pool.

Finally there are the essays. Most colleges ask kids to write some sort of personal statement—a few pages, double-spaced, explaining themselves. It's a daunting task. Not surprisingly, at the ripe old age of seventeen, many kids tend to write basically the same kinds of things: the catalog-of-achievement essay; the meaningful-activity essay (sports = life, music = life, religion = life); the community-service essay (I-spent-my-summer-in-Latin-America-and-discovered-that-poor-people-are-just-like-me); the horrible-tragedy essay (the death or illness of a friend, relative, stranger, or even dog); and the "me" essay, where they find some way to talk about themselves. Those are often the best.

At Duke, we also ask kids to write two additional short essays. Why do you want to go to Duke? In 99.9 percent of the cases, that question elicits a less than interesting response. The earnest will spit back information gleaned from our marketing materials. The gung ho will mention basketball, or more specifically "the Shot," when, in 1992, Christian Laettner fired a final-second, game-winning basket in the NCAA regional finals. Some applicants will cite a specific faculty member who's doing interesting research (that's impressive) or mention meeting an admissions officer like me who wears cool purple shoes (that's not). I argued to get rid of this essay.

The other question is about a book. Duke used to ask applicants to write about their favorite book, and we got lots of book-reportish plot summaries. So we started positing the question a little differently, asking kids to write about the way a book has "changed your understanding of yourself, the world, or other people."

We still get lots of book-reportish plot summaries. What's interesting is not so much how the kids write but which books they choose to write about. It gives you insight into the workings of the seventeen-year-old mind. (It also tells you a lot about the reading lists for Advanced Placement English courses.)

The Catcher in the Rye never seems to lose its appeal. Kids just love it when Holden Caulfield wanders around New York City denouncing phonies. One smart kid this year wrote that, when, at age twelve, he first read CITR (you tend to start abbreviating after about the 385th essay), he really identified with Holden. Part of his maturation, he wrote, was to see that he didn't want to be like Holden, after all. Holden was a jerk.

Many kids want to be like Jay Gatsby. An interesting signifier, I think, of our historical moment. The scrappy self-made (very rich) man is a hero. I don't know how they are teaching AP English classes, but a lot of kids seem to be missing the boat, at least in the harbor of East and West Egg. I went back and reread *The Great Gatsby* because I started to doubt my own memory of it. Gatsby the hero? I wasn't misremembering the book; they were misreading it.

Some students go for novels of cultural identity. Many Asian American kids write about *The Joy Luck Club*; a number of Jewish applicants write about *The Chosen or Night*. A large group of Asian Indians write about *Siddhartha*. Then there are those who choose to write about novels of nonidentity (white kids write gee-whiz essays about *Native Son*, *Invisible Man*, and any of a number of Toni Morrison books). A lot write about *Huck Finn*. This year, a valedictorian from California wrote that when he finally read Twain for himself, he realized that his mother had edited it heavily to eliminate the "racism" when she had read it to him at bedtime. It was a different book, he said.

Into Thin Air is huge. No surprise. It's a great story and appeals understandably to risk-taking teenagers. A *Prayer for Owen Meany* has long been a big hit. THE SEVENTEEN-YEAR-OLD CROWD LOVES TINY OWEN MEANY AND HIS CONTEMPORARY MORALITY TALE. Kids seem to learn about Vietnam from Tim O'Brien's *The Things They Carried* and about the Civil War from *Cold Mountain*. That they think they are learning about feminism from *Memoirs of a Geisha* kind of baffles me. Go figure.

Kids are given lots of advice on what to write in their long essay, the personal statement. They're given even more instructions on what not to write on. Nothing risky, they're told. Don't write about weakness. Or sexuality. Or experiments with drugs. Be positive. What terrible advice.

It's becoming increasingly more difficult to tell if a student has written his or her own essays. There are proliferating Web sites that will "edit" an essay for an applicant. One of my personal favorites, "EssayEdge.com," started in the dorm rooms of Harvard students, offering help and editing on the personal essay portion of the application. These students know nothing about admissions except that they were admitted. They posit a direct relationship between their own application essays and their admission to Harvard, confusing correlation with causation, a relationship that would make most admissions professionals giggle. From their Web site:

> With a three-year history of unparalleled success, EssayEdge, formerly CollegeGate, is the world's premier application essay editing service. Our professional, Harvard-educated editors do not merely offer critiques and proofing; they also provide superior editing, giving you the edge you need in the ultra-competitive college and graduate school application process. Unlike other sites, EssayEdge puts its reputation online. Please click here to view samples of our work, unsolicited customer comments, a customer poll, and descriptions of our invaluable editing services.

Though I do not doubt the commercial success of the website, the samples of their work—standard admissions essays—are perfectly mediocre, solid "threes," and would not do much for the applicant in terms of swaying an admissions decision.

Nonetheless, they list a host of options for the aspiring Ivy Leaguer: Premium Harvard-Educated Editing ($24.95+); Essay Edge Grand Service ($139.95+); Comprehensive Service ($199.95+); Second Reading; Opinion Service ($24.95+). This is relatively afford-able. Of course, when you send in your credit-card number you have no idea who will be giving you the grand, or even compre-hensive, service; how much they know about the business of read-ing applications, or even, of writing good essays. What you know, all you need to know it seems, is that whoever it is, he or she will be Harvard educated.

Except that when I sent an E-mail to them asking if I could be hired as an editor for them they said sure, and offered me twenty-five bucks a pop.

If a student doesn't believe she can write even a good rough draft of an essay, or is lazy, she could always go to ivyleaguead-missions.com. There you can buy yourself an essay: "We believe that the actual application essays from accepted Ivy League stu-dents are an invaluable resource for you. We have compiled an impressive library of them for resale. . . . We are," they boast, "all Ph.D.'s in our respective fields and have graduated from Ivy League universities." At the bottom of the text there is, of course, a note advising that they do not encourage plagiarism.

Fear's a big motivator. Smelling this, all sorts of folks are hang-ing shingles, electronic and otherwise, to capitalize on it. In terms of services offered, the focus on the personal-essay portion of the application is interesting. If you read the Web sites and the how-to books and talk to the independent counselors, there is an incredi-ble emphasis on the essay. But really, how important is it in the entirety of the process? The way in which I stressed the impor-tance of the essay while recruiting was frankly disingenuous. It was partly out of compassion for the kids. By the time they were hearing me talk, there was little they could do to bolster their candidacies, and in reality, the only part of the process over which they had complete control was in writing their essays. So I made them think it was an important thing for them to work on, if only to help them feel that they weren't helpless.

The best essays are the ones that may contain childish mistakes in grammar but are also, unmistakably, written from the heart and the mind of an intelligent kid. Be honest, I would exhort them. Write about something you care about. If you don't care about the situation in Kosovo, don't write about it. If you love your dog, write about your dog.

On the reader-rating sheet these essays, like everything else, get reduced. Why Duke? "Typ.," for typical response, which is something along the lines of great academics, great athletics. Book essays are similarly shorthanded: CITR (*Catcher in the Rye*), Gatsby, C&P (*Crime and Punishment*), P&P (*Pride and Prejudice*), etc. The personal statement also gets impersonally distilled: running = life; std. epiph (standard epiphany essay); influential teacher. Sometimes, though, an essay is so good you want to have a line to quote from it. From a summer-job essay (as a film projectionist): "When I perform perfectly, I am doing my job; when I make one tiny mistake I am a fool."

The final result, both of the student's pouring her life out into the application and then the evaluation by the first reader and the admissions officer is a string of numbers. Six numbers. Curriculum choice, achievement, recommendations, essays, personal qualities/extracurriculars, and testing. It will be presented, on the records that are generated and by the admissions officers when they talk about the kids as, say, 55433 with a 5 in testing. It's not uncommon to hear odd conversations in the offices of the second floor of the admissions office.

Says one officer to another, "Did you see that the editor of the *Duke Chronicle* just won a Rhodes Scholarship? She was a 44533—a circled four in curriculum choice, but still. Who would have thought she'd win a Rhodes?"

"Her teachers," replies the other. "They gave her a five in recs."

Or, "I just auto denied this great kid—he started his own computer company and was offered seventy-five thousand dollars to start work at Megasoft instead of going to college."

"Why did you deny him?"

"He was a 53335 with a 5 in testing."

"Oh."

At the very bottom of the reader-rating card is the summary assessment. Someone some time in the history of Duke admissions decided to call this, cleverly, the bottom line. It's where the officer writes her recommendation, either "A" for "admit," L for "waitlist," or Z for "deny," followed by a short sentence or phrase giving the reason. "A great ED admit—does everything." "Delightful, quirky—drawn to problem-solving aspects of engineering." "All recs speak to the intelligence and curiosity but do not praise the written work as much as the conversations with, ideas of." "Runner—I hope he's fast—he's gonna need it." "BWRK—no." Some of my more earnest and sentimental colleagues would use the phrase "With regret." I believe they did regret having to deny these kids.

Frequently the bottom line simply reads "NKB" Nice kid, But . . .

5

Song of Myself: *Applicants and Their Essays*

Sometimes you're the windshield; sometimes you're the bug. Run enough marathons, eventually you're going to go splat. Months of training, weeks of travel planning, tapering, crabbing at coworkers and loved ones—these are all parts of marathoning. You can plan on them. What you can't plan on is what you can't plan on. Einstein was offended by the ideas of quantum mechanics because, he said, "God does not play dice with the universe." Well, friends, the Running God does.

You could do everything "right" and wake up the morning of the race with a stomach virus. It happened to Tegla Laroupe at the Olympics. A delayed flight and you could end up spending the night before the race sleepless in an airport. Your biorhythms could be out of whack. You could commit some cosmic, karmic wrong. You could just have a bad day.

Someone must have enraged the Running God because the inaugural edition of the Raleigh Fulcrum Marathon was cursed. How often does it snow in North Carolina? Rarely. On the day before the race the weather seers were calling for a foot of snow in a state where, if there's the threat of a light dusting, everyone runs to the grocery stores and buys all the milk and bread.

Three thousand tapered, carbo-loaded, anxiety-ridden runners came to pick up their race packets and were told to come back the following week. Most of the words I heard were not fit for print. Including those coming from my own mouth.

Did it snow? Not a frigging flake.

All but about three hundred of the original entrants showed up a week later, when it was even colder and raining. The sole wheelchair entrant sped out on the course. For a mile. Then he was hit by a car. He was, fortunately, fine. His expensive chair, however, went splat.

Somewhere around mile six the police directed the lead car to turn left. The course, unfortunately, didn't turn left there. A pack of runners did. Someone figured out that the turn had been wrong, and now other runners were being directed straight ahead.

There was endless discussion afterward about the length of the suspect segment: elaborate scientific calculations, work that could be publishable in academic journals, were put forth. When people congratulated me on my time, they also asked if I was one of the cheaters.

There are a lot of variables in this 26.2-mile equation. All you can do is train hard and then cross your fingers, pour libations of Gatorade to the Running God, and hope that even if you don't run a good time, you will have a good time.

Winters in North Carolina are generally mild. It's easy to find ways to fill the days, especially when you don't have to go to work.

I could happily spend my time running, riding horses, biking, having long breakfasts reading the paper, meeting friends for coffee or lunch, taking the dog and the pig for walks around the neighborhood, and catching up on the hot new novels I've not yet read.

When interviewing for the job in admissions the opportunity to spend the months of January and February at home reading was one of the real draws. The reality is, however, that although you don't have to put on nice clothes and spend all day under fluorescent lights, you still have tons of work to do and not much time for recreation. The sun is shining outside. I am inside reading.

There are folders strewn all over my house. I pick up one and sit down on the couch. Claire Hess, from the Calhoun School. Oh yeah, my little tour guide, the girl all in black. Home address on Park Avenue. I was right, an East Sider.

Nice testing, 770 verbal, 750 math.

I remembered that the college counselor had told me that Claire would be applying early decision to Duke but she didn't, perhaps because her testing ended up being so strong.

Claire's curriculum choice at Calhoun was solid but not outstanding. She hadn't taken the hardest courses across the boards, but she had taken the highest level offered in English, history and French. She had AP biology, but no advanced chemistry or physics, and her math stopped at precalculus. Not great.

Her grades were another story. Freshman year she had done astonishingly well. This was unusual. Often there was a period of adjustment, coming to a boarding school. But she had gone to an excellent East Side middle school and was clearly well prepared and quite capable of doing the work. Sophomore year was a disaster. No grade above a B, and a smattering of Cs, even in photography. Junior year she had pulled back up to a strong B average, at a school where the best students were barely making As.

Her counselor recommendation was typically well crafted, but in Claire's case, there seemed to be genuine enthusiasm. I could tell that Becky knew Claire from more than just the required meetings that the counselors have with students. She talked about her vitality and her warmth and then went on at length about her intellectual curiosity. Not a science/math person, Claire was strong in the humanities. A good writer and a perceptive reader, she was frequently found with a book, sitting quietly away from the social hub of the school. She was partial to nineteenth-century novels, and particularly loved Jane Austen.

After a strong freshman year, Claire had medical problems sophomore year and required hospitalization. She insisted on trying to keep up with her work and inevitably her grades suffered. Her performance junior year was a much better indicator of her real potential.

She was active in the life of the school, though in a quiet kind of way. She was editor of the literary magazine, ran track and cross-country, took part in peer counseling, and tutored fifth-grade girls in math. Not a spectacular résumé for a kid applying to Duke.

She came from a high-powered New York family. She was the youngest of three kids, all of whom had gone to the Calhoun School and then on to Yale, as had generations of Hesses before them. Claire did not want to go to Yale. This caused a certain amount of strife in the family, but she had stood firm. Although she knew, her counselor said, that she would easily be admitted to Yale, and because of her spotty record she knew, too, that Duke was not a sure thing, she had still insisted on applying to Duke. She had lost the battle to apply early to Duke, and so lost, then, her best chance of getting in.

I moved on to the teacher recs. One from eleventh-grade English, the other from her senior history seminar. They both said essentially the same thing: Claire was a young woman who drove herself very hard. She was never content with an easy answer, never gave anything other than her best shot. She wanted to know the whys and hows, not just the whats. She pushed the class to a higher level; her questions sometimes unnerved other students, but she forced them to think more deeply. She would often take an unpopular stance, defend it persuasively, and end up going from being a lone voice to having the majority of her classmates agree with her position. She was a strong young woman.

Nice recs. I was warming up to this girl.

I finally got to her part 5. That's the personal part of the application, the student's own part. She described her extracurriculars, not a lot of surprises there. Then I got to the essays.

Claire's "why Duke" essay was not typical. It read, "Because it isn't Yale. That's why I want to go to Duke." She went on to describe living with the weight of six generations of Yalies and what that does to the seventeen-year-old psyche. She had not wanted to go to the Calhoun School; she was more interested in another, slightly less prestigious boarding school. But Calhoun's where the Hess family went, so that's where Claire ended up. It hadn't been the right choice for her, and she didn't want the same thing to happen with her college decision. Though she loved her family, she was different from them and wanted to have the opportunity to make different choices. Though she appreciated Yale, she knew that Duke was different. Not only did she want to get out of the Northeast, and the Ivy-centered attitude that went along with being there, she also wanted more of a balanced life. She wanted to work hard, yes, that was who she was. But she also wanted to be at a place where she could relax and have fun.

For her second short essay, the answer to the book question, Claire had chosen to write about *Pride and Prejudice*, as did probably six out of every ten girls. But Claire did a better job than most; she was a deft writer and a careful reader, just as her teachers had said.

Then came the long essay, the personal statement. Claire had attached a note to her essay. "Everyone I showed this to told me not to send it. You said in your instructions, to write on a matter of importance. This topic is, to me, a matter of life and death. I hope that I did not make a mistake in choosing to write about it."

I began reading.

"I hated the girl in the mirror. I hated her fat chipmunk cheeks, her rounded forehead, her pug nose. I hated everything about her and wanted her to go away. So I tried to make her disappear."

She wrote with a raw honesty about her struggles with anorexia. It was all making sense to me now: the hospitalization her sophomore year, the drive to perfection, the high-powered family with the high-powered expectations.

"Anyone who thinks that anorexia is about weight has never been around an anorexic. It's about power and control, it's about dealing—or not dealing—with issues of sexuality, it's about per-

116

fection and self-hatred. It takes a lot of energy to hate yourself this much."

By the time I got to the last paragraph I was crying.

"My weight is now, and has been for the past year and a half, in the range of what is considered normal. In this age of Kate Moss and Ally McBeal, that's still pretty skinny. I am able to eat these days without doing higher math. Am I cured? I suspect I will never be cured. I will always have to eat and thus I will always have to struggle with issues around eating."

I wade through a bunch of auto denies. I can guess that they will be auto denies because their test scores, rank in class, and number of AP courses they have taken have already been noted by the first readers on the "jackets" holding their files. At a glance I can see that these kids have no chance.

The kids at the top and the bottom of the pool do not go into committee. At the start of each reading season, the director sets the "auto" parameters. After each application is read, the reader ratings get summed. The three from the first reader are combined with the three from the admissions officer, and the two additional ratings for essays and extracurriculars are doubled. Those ratings are combined with a doubled rating for testing. The highest possible sum is sixty—ten points for each of the ratings for curriculum choice, achievement, recommendations, personal qualities/extracurriculars, essays, and testing. We often refer to kids by their sum: "A fifty-four sum—she was awesome." At least that's the way it's done for the college of arts and science. For engineers the total possible sum is one hundred. The testing rating is tripled (with more emphasis placed on the math score); curriculum choice and achievement are both doubled. This means an engineering applicant can be admitted with unextraordinary extracurriculars and having written a bad essay; they tend to be good testers and dull.

For the college of arts and sciences, the auto deny sum is usually around forty-seven. The admissions officer reads the file, computes the sum, and then, assuming the applicant is not compelling, puts the folder in the office of an associate director who signs off on the deny (perhaps briefly looking over the folder), the decision goes into the computer, and a letter is generated to be stuffed into a thin envelope.

An applicant may be auto admitted with a sum of fifty-two and above, provided they also have a five in testing (above 1480). There are applicants who meet those criteria whom you don't want to auto admit. They may have done everything right: taken all the hard courses and done well, gotten high scores on their standardized tests, and their teachers find them diligent and hardworking. If you don't like a kid, for whatever reason, it's easy to keep them out. But for those you love, for the very top of the applicants, there has been a program to let them know, early on in the process that they are likely to be admitted.

They are sent a "likely letter" from the director, telling them that we have read their application and that they are in the top tier of our applicants. Providing they continue to perform at the same level, they can expect to be admitted in April. These letters can lead to confusion. Applicants, parents, and college counselors call wanting to know what they mean. They mean, we tell them, exactly what they say. As long as the student doesn't start failing calculus or robbing banks, she should consider herself admitted. It's a way of gaining some good feeling from the top kids—letting them know before anyone else does that we want them. We are not the only school that sends out likely letters.

Although you can't usually tell an auto admit just from looking at the jacket, it's generally easy to spot an auto deny. I pick up the jacket for Elizabeth Manteo, Almaden High School. Her grade grid shows improvement: Seven As and two Bs freshman year; eight As one B+ sophomore year; straight As junior year in three honors and one AP class. Senior year she is taking four APs. She has a 4.36 weighted GPA and her class rank is 34 out of 358, shared by 5 other students. Her guidance counselor says that she is a "class leader, excellent creative talent and athletic ability; well qualified, powerful candidate." AP English: "the rarest of academically superior students, upper 5 percent of AP class; has tools necessary to excel." AP U.S. history: "one of best all around in eighteen years; athletic, warm and compassionate, respected." This guy is, it turns out, also her crew coach. Her ECs were four years of crew, three of cross-country, vice president of Amnesty International; Big Brothers and Sisters. Essays: typical "why Duke"; book is about schoolgirls and their low sense of self-esteem; long essay about work in leper colony in Egypt. They are better than average, show some insight, and show her to be a neat kid and a good person. SAT Is: verbal 640; math 610. SAT IIs: writing 650; calculus (IC): 660; biology 580.

She's a 53333 with a 2 in testing. A thirty-eight sum. An auto deny.

Next. Michael Todd, from a rural western Massachusetts public school, 67 percent college bound. ninth: seven As, three Bs; tenth: six As, one C; eleventh: two As, five Bs. Ten APs offered in the school, Sean took only one last year and is taking AP English this year. A weak curriculum. His GPA is 3.8 out of 4.0, his rank 25 out of 256. Counselor: "Does not follow crowd, top 2 percent in charms and personality, excellent speech and writing talent." English: "bright, refreshingly open, candid, love of learning, solid reader and writer." U.S. history: "infectious stance on human rights, has become conscience of the class." ECs: Vball 3, Science Olympiad 3 (VP this year), Model Congress, Boys State. Book essay on *All the Pretty Horses*; long essay, not impressive on a conservation project. Testing: verbal 710, math 750. Dad is unemployed; mom is computer programmer.

I like this kid. Then I add up the numbers. A thirty-five sum. No way would he make it through committee. Into the heap of auto denies.

Charles High School, an excellent public school in an affluent Boston suburb, has sent me Elaine Meyer. She's taken four APs out of the full range the school offers. Her grades are As and Bs. It's hard to tell exactly where she falls in the class, since the school has it's own peculiar grading scale (out of 11 points, she has an 8.1) and they do not, of course, rank. There is no counselor rec from this school, instead a sheaf of short comments from a host of teachers. European history: "quiet gentle manner—wonderful addition to any classroom—developing her writing skills." English: "quiet, but gets her ideas across, hardworking, diligent, determined." Wrote on *Tuesdays with Morrie*; long essay on trip to Israel and her friendship with an Arab girl. Typical, average writing, no real insight. ECs: a skater. She'd done figure skating for nine years and is nationally ranked; founded the ice hockey team at the school (there are two other girls on the team); Hebrew high school, Ukrainian dance club. Testing: verbal 700, math 680. Dad is a rabbi with a Ph.D. from Yale.

Bottom line: NKB. Nice Kid But . . . Z.

Amber Wang, Stanford High School. Six APs taken in high school, scored five on psychology, four on AB calc, and two on stats. Two summer-school classes at Stanford University. Grades stink. Ninth: two, five, and two. Tenth: six and five; eleventh: six, seven, and one. She is in the third decile of the class. Cnslr: "throws herself into the courses she loves, a will of iron, has the drive to accomplish." AP calc: "conscientious, there were times she might have taken a stronger interest in material, neither exceptional skill for testing nor affinity for math." AP psych: "held her own, interest in equal rights." ECs: Key Club, 4; Youth and Government, 4; Safe Rides, pres; church youth group, 4; varsity track, 4; varsity bball, 4; Pres and cofounder of Human Rights Club. Essays: *Waiting for Godot*; long essay on feng shui. Nice attempt, failed execution. Testing: verbal 760, math 740.

Clearly an underachiever. Too bad, I liked her. Auto deny.

David Armstrong, Buford School. So much for the easy reads. Buford, like many of the elite boarding schools, does its grading idiosyncratically. And of course, none of the courses are listed as APs. So I have to think about this one.

Young David has a solid 86.3 average. That makes him pretty darn average in our pool. A B student, at best. His course load is also average. He is not taking the hard senior seminars this year, last year he took a fairly light load. He did take the AP history exam last year and scored a four; I would expect that after having taking the standard Buford junior history course. Cnslr: "David is "cool" because of his background, looks, and athleticism—his honesty, modesty, and compassion set him apart. He strives for inclusivity—makes tough decisions." Physics: "among the most persistent—willing to be responsible—too hard on self." Eng: "natural leader, determined, seeks challenges, worked consistently and enthusiastically." They clearly like him, perhaps are charmed by him. By these recs damn him. He's no academic superstar. ECs: head of community service board; head tour guide; captain of lacrosse; captain of water polo; recipient of the Columbia Book Award; head of Green Key Society. Book: *Walden*. Eschewing greed. Long, rambling essay about his decision to quit football, an account of morphing from a boy to a man. I'm not convinced. Testing: verbal 680, math 710. Dad is an investment banker; mom is an executive at a recruiting firm. Parents are separated; home is Upper East Side of Manhattan, with mom.

This is the classic Branford guy. Life, I think, will be easy for him. But it will not be at Duke. Z.

Next is a Calhoun kid, James Carlson. I remember seeing him when I was up there. I remember him because he was the only African American guy in the room. We'd chatted briefly—he was a football player, though had no interest in playing for Duke. I'd been looking forward to seeing his application, and here it was. It was wonderful. He'd taken four AP tests and had scored three fives and a four. His grades put him at the top of the group applying from the school. His recs were fives, unusual for Calhoun: "one of the most talented Calhoun has produced in years, maturity beyond years, one of very few who were outstanding scholars, top athletes, and wonderful people." His English teacher said James was "full of wonder and desire to understand, remarkable writing skills, one of the most interesting thinkers ever." He was the captain of both football and baseball, a dorm prefect, played sax, and worked in the school's dining hall. His book essay was on Lorene Cary's *Black Ice*, an account of being one of the first African Americans at one of the fancy boarding schools, and his long essay was football = life, but he traced the game back to the *Iliad*. James was on a scholarship through Prep for Prep, a program that takes kids out of their city schools and prepares them for—and then sends them off to—elite prep schools. His testing was verbal 670, math 680. His dad's whereabouts were unknown, his mom was a seamstress. He was a "fee waiver," which means that he had shown that paying the sixty-dollar application fee would be a hardship for his family. I put him through as an auto admit—the auto admit sums were lower for African-Americans and Latino applicants—and made a note to the African American recruiter that James should be one of the dozen or so kids who were flown in for the black student weekend. We didn't want this one to get away.

John Osborne. Norwich High School. Straight As. Taken eight out of twelve APs. Ranked 3 out of 292. Four fives on the three AP tests he's taken so far. Cnslr: "one of the outstanding student-athletes at Norwich. Teachers use superlatives to describe him." History: "in thirty-two years of teaching, one of the most intellectually gifted student I ever taught. Written work shows a breadth far exceeding a high school senior." No other recs, but the file is considered complete. ECs: National Honor Society pres; tennis, 4, capt; junior and senior class pres; church group; works twenty hours a week at the Gap; Archery! Apparently young John came in fourth at the National Junior Olympics in archery. Cool.

Since he used the common application, we don't have his specific Duke essays, just the long essay, which is, not surprisingly along the lines of "archery = life." In order to admit him we will need this supplement. Not so much for the essays, but to make sure he has answered the question about any disciplinary actions that may have been taken against him. Testing: 790, 800.

He's a 55534 with a 5 in testing—a fifty-four sum. I put this young man through as an auto admit.

Another north of Boston kid, from another affluent suburb, Margaret Janus has taken no AP classes of the sixteen that are offered, and has only taken two honors classes. Her grades are a mix of As and Bs. Her counselor mentions her commitment to excel. Her math teacher says that "she is not mathematically creative, but is motivated and excels in field hockey." History says she needs to be more of a presence in class, and to be less focused on grades. She played field hockey all four years of high school and played in the band as well. Testing was 590, 570. As I was about to write Z on the bottom line I realized that this girl would be coming back to haunt me: both parents had gone to Duke.

I wade through a large number of auto denies—all in the top 10 percent of their class, with mostly As on their transcripts. SATs are usually in the high six hundreds to low seven hundreds. Their teachers and counselors will be surprised that they do not get into Duke. These same kids, even ten years ago, probably would have been admitted. But on their reader-rating cards they are threes and fours. Standard, typical BWRKs. Good, just not good enough.

Carolyn Hass, from Silicon Valley High School had taken a full IB diploma course. She was ranked 2 out of 320, all As. Testing was 780, 730. Counselor and teacher recs were outstanding. She was a ballet dancer and devoted an unbelievable amount of time not only to dancing, but to commuting to her classes. Her essays were good, but not great. She was a fifty-two sum, but I didn't want to put her through as an auto admit. I liked her, a lot, but I didn't love her. She'd be discussed in committee, and by then I'd have a better sense of how she stacked up against the other kids.

Cheryl Conrad was a different story. She had six eight hundreds and eight fives on AP tests. She'd taken courses at the University of Massachusetts, Amherst, in math and physics since eighth grade. She'd done her one research on nonlinear dynamics. She also worked twenty hours a week at the Gap and had produced her own musical in her high school. She was a cheerleader. This was my kind of cheerleader. I put her through as an auto admit and nominated her for the top academic scholarship.

I start making a collection of my favorite essays. I like to be able to talk about ones that work when I'm giving group information sessions or visiting schools. I've gotten quite a nice sheaf of them at this point.

My car and I are a lot alike. . . .

I drive a 1986 Buick Century. My family won this car in the summer of 1986 at the St. Jude's Church raffle. I must be a privileged teenager because I have a car at my disposal whenever I want it. Nice try. True enough, my car would fall under a loose definition of transportation, but it is also true that no one else in my family is willing to drive it for fear that it won't make it out of the driveway. This 1986 is purple and maroon, with a hint of gold (the rust). Every time I slam the trunk shut, the back end loses a small portion of its structure. The left radio speaker is broken. The roof leaks every time it rains. The power steering rarely works and I cannot unlock the driver's side door. The Buick accelerates from zero to sixty in . . . , well, to tell the truth, it never gets up to sixty. If it did, my estimation would be about ten minutes. The defrost system is broken. When I turn on the heat it smells like a dead animal. And the fuel gauge is dysfunctional. You are probably wondering, "How did this pile of junk pass inspection?" Good question. I'm guessing that Divine Intervention had a role.

When it is cold (for the Buick this is anything under forty degrees), my car has a fifty percent starting rate, which, may I add, is rapidly declining. In the winter, I have to start the car before I take a shower so that it is ready to go when I am. In the morning before school, I don't have to beep for my friends because they can hear my car coming down the road. I use the Buick as a locker room, a book bag, a closet, and a garbage can. In the school parking lot, there aren't fifty Buicks, there are forty-nine Buicks and the Buick. My friends pity me. My sisters refuse to drive it. My parents always remind me, "You can thank your lucky stars you have a car. Do you know how many kids your age have to walk two miles to school through the driving snow and . . ." You know where that one goes.

So what makes this car so special? My answer, in one simple

word: everything. The Buick has character, made-in-America durability, and a history of good times and happy memories. It greets me at the end of each day, good or bad; it shares those initial moments of solitude and transition. Perhaps its most redeeming quality is that my music has never stopped. The tape player and radio still work.

If you want to know who I am, take one look at the character of this beat up, worn down piece of junk. I'm not perfect, no one is. But like the Buick, I'm built to last. I don't worry about the small stuff. I appreciate everything I have and cherish all that I accomplish. Most importantly, I'm honest. Just like the Buick, I come in the package you see. I am proud of who I am and for what I stand. In a sense, the Buick and I reflect each other. My car may not be the best piece of machinery on the road, but it sure does get the job done. So do I.

The photograph of my Grandma Luisa Sazueta, who left our lives a few years ago, sits on my dresser. Her pensive, resolute, and serious gaze implores me to remember my promises to her that I would become everything that she could not be and that I would take on the responsibility of her ideals: the sacredness of family unity, the maintenance of our language and culture, the primariness of education, the centrality of a political consciousness and the willingness to commit to social action, the belief in positive thinking and hard work as springboards to success, and the dedication to the equality of women. All of that and more is my Grandmother's legacy to me. She was the matriarch of our extended family and the center of my life as I was growing up. My Grandma was a curious blend of the most modern ideas and the most timeless understandings of life and its meanings. As I study my Grandma's photo, I am struck by her natural beauty, her sophistication and carriage, by her self confidence, well put together visage, and obvious good taste. She was the provocative blend of the sweet café con leche that she drank and the pungent brilliant red chile that she prepared. She was warm and loving, yet decisive and commanding when the time called for it. She embraced new ideas as passionately as she cherished the old, simple folk ways she grew up with on a small ranch in Sonora, Mexico. She selected from the old and the new those ideas that seemed worthwhile, never forgetting or putting aside old values because they were old, and never fearing new ideas because of their unfamiliarity. This is a woman of remarkable courage, stamina, and native intelligence, a real feminist in the true sense of the word, and a pillar of strength, integrity and compassion—the architect of my life.

On a melting Italian afternoon in July, our rental car steamed into town, its inside temperature 108, the wide-open windows offering no relief, the tree-lined road a mirage of cool. Watching the scenery pass by, I was jolted out of my stupor: Was that the Leaning Tower of Pisa? I blinked and straightened up for another look. Oh, what a sight! The leaning tower, which had shared a corner of my childhood with Willy Wonka's Chocolate Factory and an old house in Paris that was covered with vines, was real. It was also really leaning. At that moment, my commitment to perfection began to crumble.

The building, a bell tower for Pisa Cathedral, was begun in 1174, but the soft soil beneath it began to sink after the third story was added. Construction was halted for a period of head-scratching, after which the stone cutters picked up their tools and the masons went back to work. Why did they carry on? They couldn't have foreseen that their tower would be leaning, or even still standing, eight centuries later. Perhaps they valued their faulty tower simply because it was their work, and so they kept building, stone by stone.

Well, the ground has been shifting under my feet lately, and I'm leaning a bit, too. I've been thinking about my life: examining its beauty and its imperfections, pausing to evaluate my passions and my resources, and reflecting on the work I've done and the work ahead.

In my family, I've felt the pain of my parents' divorce and my mother's serious illness. I've also experienced the sweetness of unconditional love, the healing of forgiveness and compassion, the joy of a great conversation, the soul-rocking pleasure of music, and the power of humor. At school, I've had great teachers to encourage my curiosity, to inspire me to think, and to haul me up short if I'm tempted to take the safe rather than the risky path. In my community, I've been angered by the growing economic imbalances that can squash the dreams of children, and I've found reason for hope by tutoring some of those children—by seeing how easy it is to hold out my hand and help someone bridge the gap.

In my seventeen years, I've struggled with shyness and control-freak tendencies. What's a perfectionist to do? I jumped into mosh pits, joined speech teams, acted in plays and musicals, helped out other kids with their homework, learned to be a good listener, covered one of my bedroom wall with words, hung sparkly things from my ceiling, and let laundry and books pile up until I had to tunnel my way out. I'm more relaxed these days, although I still have trouble ordering pizza over the phone.

Ordering spaghetti in Piazza Navona—that one I can do. Two of the best gifts life has given me are my grandparents, who live in Scotland, and who have taken me traveling with my brother and sister. Let me tell you: Auntie Mame has nothing on Granny Jo and Franpa. We've waltzed in Salzburg, vogued with the Three Graces at the Louvre, and listened to the silence at Culloden and Bastogne. These travels, more than any history book, have taught me how wonderfully creative—and how insanely destructive—humans can be. The Earth has been my teacher, too: lessons in gratitude and humility as I breathed the thin air atop the Zugspitze, splashed through a burn in a Scottish glen, or smelled the rain as it washed the sky above Amsterdam.

The next stop on my journey will be college, and this year of transition has its own beauties and imperfections. I'm taking six killer classes, wrestling with huge choices, and wondering how sad it will be to leave home. On the other hand, I'm finding my groove in calculus, enjoying my family and friends more than ever, and feeling the thrill of possiblity. There's so much to learn, to feel, and to do; my work has barely begun. So I'll keep building, just as the people of Pisa did. If a few cracks appear, I'll try not to worry, because you never know what might add to the depth and beauty of a life. My tools are ready. Hand me the next stone.

As I belly-danced with her at the night club on our first evening in Ankara, I knew I had made the right decision. But when my friends first discovered that I would be going to Turkey with her for a week and a half, they told me I was being ridiculous. They couldn't believe I would be spending more than a week traveling with an older woman, even though they knew how much I liked her. I considered their warnings, but in the end ignored them. I had really been looking forward to the trip, and nothing was going to stop me from going with her.

As it turned out, those ten days I spent in Turkey with my grandmother this summer were some of the most special of my life. I was able to visit the country of her birth and spend time with someone who has meant so much to me over the years. My grandmother has been a crucial figure in my life, both as a role model and as a friend.

The more I am with her, the more I come to admire her outlook on life. She is 82 years old, but acts and feels 40 years younger. She plays tennis regularly, often with the third-ranked player in the 80 and over division. Last year she started playing golf, and since then it has become a passion of hers. She figures that she should be able to do everything she used to, despite slightly arthritic joints, and just as well as when she was 50 years younger. For me at the age of 17, it is hard to imagine being limited in my physical abilities, but I do realize that at her age her vivacity is something special. Recently in New York, my father and I took her to her first professional baseball game and, though she did not exactly fit in with her neatly ironed pants, buttoned-down shirt, and Sunday New York Times (it was a double-header), I was thrilled to have her come. And when there was a question over whether we should go to Turkey this summer despite the risk of terrorism following the death sentence of Ocalan (prior to the devastating earthquake), she did not hesitate to say we should go. She thought there are few opportunities like this over a lifetime, and the chance was worth taking.

Both through listening to and observing my grandmother, I have learned my most important lesson: make the most of every day and every opportunity. Usually she stays up until two o'clock every night and wakes up at 7:00 because she feels that sleeping is a waste of time. Like her, I am a night owl, though when I don't have school the next morning, I am apt to sleep until noon.

Aside from her lessons on life, she has played an important role in stimulating my intellectual side. While I devoured Hardy Boys books in elementary school, she read me Robert Louis Stevenson, Dickens and Greek myths. Since she is an accomplished writer and voracious reader, I have always enjoyed discussing literature with her. If a question arises at 1:30 in the morning when I am studying for an English test on *The Great Gatsby* or *Macbeth*, it is she whom I call. It was my grandmother who tore me away from Candyland and Chutes and Ladders and introduced me to Scrabble, and whose phenomenal vocabulary, in part, inspired me to put my mind to learning new words.

She has been equally important in encouraging my interest in art. When I was younger I loved to sit down and draw, and while my attempts at realism generally led to tears, she was always support-ive and in particular praised my abstract designs. This meant a lot to me coming from her; she is a talented artist, unlike my parents, who readily admit that their artistic development was arrested sometime around kindergarten. When a slot opened at the last minute for a school-sponsored trip to Tuscany, my grandmother encouraged me to go despite the previously planned trip to Turkey. In fact, the trip was an outstanding experience, as I had a chance to spend hours each day for nearly three weeks drawing amidst a picturesque land-scape. Although during the school year I am usually too busy to sit down and draw for any extended period of time, in my free time it is still something I deeply enjoy doing.

Over the years, she has not only been a superb mentor but simply a wonderful person to be around. Kind, dedicated, and quick to point out the lighter side of life, she has many ideal characteristics that I try to emulate. Though I am never going to be as perpetually optimistic as she, or may never have the same incredible zest for life that she has, I at least have a wonderful role model. To me, she has the spirit of a teenager, even though she still often confuses Michael Jordan and Michael Jackson.

So, just exactly who am I? I am a hard worker who could also win medals for my amazing ability at procrastination. I favor compassion over righteousness, and am addicted to the instant messenger. I love James Taylor and Dave Matthews Band, especially when Dave sings, "You wear nothing but you wear it so well." I want the best education I can get and want to continue learning throughout life. I wish I could understand people better, know what makes them laugh, cry, love and hate. I am Pete Sampras' biggest fan. I would rather be seen as faithful than Christian. I love deeply and honestly and I hate jealousy although I have been jealous many a time or two. I crave Ben & Jerry's Chunky Monkey ice cream like some heroin addicts crave their next hit. I wish I'd been 18 in 1969. I love to dream big, to talk and to sleep. Most importantly, I want to go to college.

What situations have influenced me? First, I have never met my father. I don't know the color of his eyes, the smell or his cologne, or the reflections in his laughter. I once felt part of me was missing along with the missing knowledge of this man. However, I realize now that the person I am is complete and has been shaped by other people in my life who have treated me better than I could have ever deserved.

Also, I am poor. Although most people would rather die than not have money, being poor has taught me the value of a dollar. I know what it is like when the rent can not be paid or the electricity has been cut off. I also know what it is like to depend on the kindness of family even to the point where one's pride is trampled upon and eventually pushed aside.

My life has been harder than many of my peers, but I have been given so many blessings. I value my intellect and personality. I value my faults. My only hope is for opportunity.

When I open the front door, the surprising aroma of crushed chili peppers, garlic, onions, and cabbage greets me. Normally, I would go to the kitchen to find out what my mom is cooking. Instead, I go to the garage. That combination of smells can only mean one thing: my mom is making kimchi. As I get closer to the garage, I hear the laughter of the women from my church; they may be getting ready for a women's association bazaar. I open the door to be met by the glare of hundreds of empty jars waiting to be filled to the brim with kimchi.

With a kiss on the cheek, my mom hands me a knife, a peeler, and a checkal (a device that chops vegetables into julienne pieces) and points to a pile of turnips and carrots. Since I was five, my job has been to peel the carrots and turnips and julienne them. Now that I'm seventeen, nothing has changed.

Most young boys spend quality time with their fathers cheering at baseball games or learning how to play football. I, however, spend time in the kitchen with my mom. I have learned how to make everything from kimchi to rice cakes to marinated beef to traditional dumplings. Of course I started out peeling vegetables—mostly garlic—when I was younger. Then as I got older, my mom let me stir food that was cooking on the stove. Now, I make whole dishes myself. (There is a running joke among the church women that I will have a hard time finding a wife because she will be frustrated when I do the womanly things better than she does.) While we cooked together, my mom would talk to me about everything you could possibly imagine, ranging from funny childhood events to heart-aching stories. The kitchen with its familiar fragrances of steaming rice, garlic, hot peppers, and simmering soup provides a warm environment that facilitates conversations between mother and son. I cherish these talks so much because living in a Korean family does not allow such talks very often. The Korean culture encompasses hidden love and secret sacrifices. With my mom in the kitchen, it is different. She lets go of her inhibition and through the years has revealed her life to me. Because my mom openly spoke to me, I began to open up also. I started to let her know how I felt about school and all the things that plague adolescents, namely girls. The discussions on dating, marriage, girls, and sex were never uncomfortable because my mom always found a way to make me laugh about them. (Once my mom said to me in a thick Korean accent, "Every time you have sex, I want you to make sure and use a "condo." I instantly burst into laughter and said, "Mom, that could get kind of expensive!" That one little mispronunciation made everything less awkward.) Soon we had developed a lasting bond.

I would never have known what an extraordinary woman my mother is if we had not started to cook together. She tells me that I'm the only one of her children to learn the family recipes and the stories of her life. While I will not have all the same ingredients when I am away at college, the recipes will remain a part of me always.

I became a card-carrying member of the American Civil Liberties Union about a year ago, after my school literary magazine stared down a censorship threat from the administration. My decision to join this much-maligned organization was not easy. I barely had the money, for one thing, and I was wryly nervous about killing my (non-existent) political aspirations before I was old enough to vote. Lest you think my apprehensions were exaggerated, consider what happened to Michael Dukakis in 1988 after he was accused of belonging to the ACLU; even today a certain McCarthyist congressman is fond of asking prospective federal judges "Are you now, or have you ever been, a member of the ACLU?" So even though I couldn't see myself running for president or sitting on the federal bench, I was a bit leery of joining such an unpopular crowd.

More important, though, was the fact that I disagreed deeply with the official ACLU position on many, many issues. I still do. As a caring human being I see little harm in letting vicious, incurable, perverted rapists rot in jail, and as a white college applicant I'm selfishly uncomfortable with affirmative action programs which seem dangerously close to quotas—two beliefs contrary to the ACLU party line. Why, then, did I become a member if I disagree with the organization?

The simple answer is based on principle: I believe in the Bill of Rights and I want the freedoms guaranteed there to remain intact for myself and for future generations of Americans. You say the ACLU is dedicated to preserving those freedoms? Great. Take my $20 and mail me my card. Simple as that.

The more complex answer is, well, complex. Part of it, certainly, is the sheer orneriness allegedly present in all teenagers. In the course of the censorship skirmish I mentioned at the beginning of this essay, I discovered an illicit truth: there are few things more satisfying than being told you can't say something and then proving you damn well can, thank you. In this way, joining the ACLU was, broadly speaking, a benign way of exorcising my inner rebel—less painful than getting a nose ring, more sensible than suddenly flunking all my classes, less damaging to my hearing than listening to obnoxious music and a great deal smarter than cultivating marijuana.

Then, too, I have always had a deep sense of fairness; I wouldn't be at all surprised if my first words after "mama" and "dada" were "It's not fair!" I always hated the old "life isn't fair" bromide, even as I came to accept it as an unfortunate truth. Given this background, it's not hard to see that in my mind, by defending the constitutional rights of everyone, even the rotten dregs of humanity—rapists, Satanists, Nazis and worse—the ACLU is being scrupulously, even painfully, fair. I have to admire that kind of devotion to constitutional justice, that kind of absolute integrity, even as I shudder at what it might lead to.

Finally, I admire what the ACLU does despite our differing views because I believe that someone must take on the odious task of protecting the rights of the hateful, the lewd, the morally abhorrent and the just plain unpopular, lest we lose our own freedoms through negligence or hypocrisy. In this matter, the ACLU and I are entirely in agreement, and that, for me, is what counts.

My father is an Aquarius. My mother, his ex-wife, likes to use this astrological information to explain his thrill seeking trips to Antarctica and Tanzania, and to discern why he has fathered five children who range from eleven months to thirty years in age. She says he follows his own direction, something that most Aquarii do.

I am a Cancer. I would rather spend my days watching rental movies while bundled up on the couch than backpacking in the Himalayan mountains.

As a gift for my thirteenth birthday my father brought me to Portugal, a destination that was a compromise for the two of us: it was not the usual European trip, which made my father happy. However, Portugal was not so remote that I couldn't find it on a map, a security that eased my fears of an avalanche swallowing us. Spending two weeks alone with the man who once walked through a field with deerflies on his head because he didn't want to disturb them was not appealing to me. Nonetheless, I thought that the trip might possibly act as a catalyst to mend our fragmented relationship. What I did not realize was that we would arrive back in Boston barely speaking because I would not "play" with him by talking to the Portuguese people and submerging myself in the culture. I was thirteen, uninterested in lifting my eyes from the books that I had brought along.

Through my travel experiences with my father I have learned a great deal about our relationship. While he likes to eat burritos at the local taco stand in Mexico, I would rather eat dinner at home with a small group of friends. Our vastly different outlooks on life produce problems when we are alone together for a long time; one of us usually leaves with wounded feelings. My father likes to experiment with new cultures and people, while I prefer to cling onto the old ones that I have finally begun to trust. I find comfort in the familiar; he seeks adventure in the unexplored.

Most of the time my father does not understand how I act, saying that I need to take more risks and stop "bottling up" my feelings. He thinks I do not love him when I decline his challenges, and claims that I do not have the time for him. Just once, he has said, he would like to see me consider something he has to say. Hearing this line leave his lips, I often smile inside, wondering if he will ever realize how much his uninhibited spirit makes me want to come out of my crab shell and run wild in the African meadows. Though I always defend myself, I know that many of his insights into my timidity are correct. It's funny that he thinks I am trying to become the opposite of who he is. In reality, sometimes I'd love to have been born under his sign.

6

Much Madness Is Divinest Sense: *Alumni Interviews and Counselor Interventions*

When I moved to Durham eight years ago, people spoke about Atlantic Coast Conference basketball—particularly Duke basketball—like it was a virus: You come here, you catch it. For seven years, I was immune. I embraced my basketball antipathy. I reveled in my resistance.

Then I, too, became infected. The vector was Trajan Langdon, captain of Duke's team. I met him, liked him, began to watch him play. I stopped turning away the prized Duke basketball tickets that I was occasionally offered. I started screaming at the television, complaining about the announcers, cursing the referees. I became a fan.

Many of my friends are basketball fans, and a number are devoted followers of the Duke women's team. So I started going to women's games this year. In so doing, I've found a rich diversity. Part of the reason I'm still such an ignorant spectator is that my focus is often elsewhere, like on who else is watching. At a women's game, I take my seat in the most mixed crowd I am ever in. I am thrilled to be hanging with a critical mass of lesbians. I like being in a place where interracial couples feel comfortable. I enjoy watching fathers bring packs of daughters and their friends. For less than the price of a movie ticket, families from the wider Durham community show up as well. The Gee Whiz program buses in middle-school girls. Sitting in this diverse crowd, I get chills.

In some ways, I think, collegiate women's basketball—both its athletes and its fans—represents an imagined future. I do also watch the game (though I still never seem to know why the refs are blowing the whistle). The women's ball is slightly smaller than the men's, and the women's game is different. It's slower. You don't get those outrageous bursts of athletic power, players flying through the air. What you do see is five people working together. There's less showboating, more passing. A friend who coaches a girl's middle-school team says girls are afraid of being seen as "ball hogs" and will go out of their way to avoid such an accusation. That means less aggressive but more cohesive play. All that feminist-theory stuff about the differences in women's ways of being—nonhierarchical, seeking connection—in full-court action.

If you ask people why they go to the women's games, they say it's about the fundamentals of basketball. It's pure, it's essential, it's the way the game was meant to be played, the way it was played by men twenty years ago. The women shoot as well as the men, and do better, percentage-wise, on free throws. I can't help believing that the next generation, the little girls who are being bused in, will think it's cool to spend time practicing their shooting and passing and that the women's game will become even more about finesse, about precision.

The Duke men's players show up for many of the women's home games. I love that they come, though it also troubles me that their appearance automatically takes attention away from the women's game. When the men show up, tiny autograph seekers mob them. Seeing those tall men surrounded by swarms of kids is a hoot. It is also troubling. The young boys engage the players, chat. But the girls seem only to want proximity. They sit near the players in passive, silent, benevolent adoration. They admire the women; they revere the men.

Before one game, I trotted over to ask one of the male players what he liked about the women's games. He said women's basketball was still "unclouded by commercialism." Ironic, I thought, from someone who is likely, in the near future, to profit enormously from the commercialism of the sport. My own hope is that, in time, women's basketball will become more commercial. I want to see women's games sell out; I'd like to see women players on TV commercials and cereal boxes; I'd love to see even more young girls grow up with hoop dreams.

While our most popular men's sports are all about big teams—football, basketball, baseball, hockey—until recently, women's athletics has focused on individuals—think of gymnastics, figure skating, tennis, golf. At this point, the women athletes we know best, we know as individuals, not as members of a team. We are used to having the cameras focus on one female body, in a tennis skirt or skin-tight costume. We want feminized, personal relationships with our female athletes. We want them to be both/and—both athletes and women who fill traditional roles as girlfriends (of men), wives, and mothers. We don't want them to be tough or crude or brazen off the playing field. With the men, as long as they're not committing murder or saying racist things in public, we don't hear that much—at least during the games, in the "color commentary"—about what they do in private.

As I sit in Cameron Indoor Stadium watching the Duke women's basketball games, I find myself thinking that this is an important historical moment, that the world is changing right in front of me. Afterward, the little girls rush the players and ask for autographs. They lean over to slap hands as the women run off the court. They can grow up seeing sports as something to aspire to, to reach for, to grow toward. These youngsters don't know that women have been allowed to play basketball in this arena for only the past twenty-five years; they don't know about life before Title IX, and they can't imagine how different things were for their own mothers and, more, for their grandmothers. Yes, the world sure is changing. At this moment, I'm glad to be a spectator.

I always thought that February, not April, was the cruelest month. I haven't been getting out much lately, aside from basketball breaks—watching the men's games on television and the women's games in Cameron—I've been doing almost nothing but reading applications. It's getting tiresome. I'm getting tired. The kids are starting to look even more alike. Since most of the high testers have already been read and sent likely letters, what remains are, well, the remains. Lots of BWRKs, lots of auto denies.

I go into work, though infrequently. When I arrive this morning I find on my desk a stack of alumni interview forms. They are arranged in no order whatsoever, neither alphabetical nor even by state. I am responsible for placing these in the files of my applicants, if I chose to do so. Leafing through them I can see that they will be of little or no help to me. The applicants are evaluated on a scale of one to five. Most of them receive threes from their Duke alumni interviewers—"Solid."

I decide to buckle down and read through them in one marathon session.

"Sarah has no prominent interests outside of academic life except for movies. She is a very sweet young lady and had many questions about size, environment, weather, however I do not feel she is as outstanding as applicants that I have previously interviewed."

"Patrick is a nice looking applicant. Very physically rock hard mountain biking fit. Brother's going to MIT and Georgetown. Seems to be hardworking, energetic, and enthusiastic. His knowledge of public current events did not seem very broad. No surprises here, this guy wants to get into Duke and learn as much as possible."

"Nice house, nestled in curvy roads of hilly Hillandale, one of the most expensive areas in San Francisco. Father is a patent attorney and came up under discussion of personal heroes. Matthew is a blasé kid, a wiry athlete type not oozing with questions and enthusiasm. He is applying to a lot of colleges and is not clear on what he wants from a college or where he wants to go. I do not think he will be going to Duke."

"Norman Henson: 1) Interesting person; 2) Mature for his age; 3) Seems to have thought out his life's goals and ambitions well."

"Deanne is a very cute girl who has a lot of energy and enthusiasm. She seems very serious about her schoolwork and takes pride in her academic achievements. There is a good balance of academic, athletic, and service-oriented activities. She gets a lot of enjoyment from her extracurricular activities and will go out of her way to attempt to involve others in a nonthreatening way. She seems very organized and compulsive about her schoolwork. If I had one reservation, it would be that she seems to come from a very sheltered home life and may be a bit more immature than some of her peers that I have interviewed. I would recommend her as an excellent candidate."

"Jeff was relaxed and natural in the interview, an impressive quality in that stressful situation. However, I was disappointed in the shallowness of our conversation. He didn't seem able or eager to discuss things at an abstract level. When asked to name an intellectual discovery which piqued his interest, he had no answer, even when I gave him a lengthy example to give him time to think. He also had NO questions for me about Duke, which to me is a deal breaker."

"Brian was not a very enthusiastic applicant, and showed little real interest in either the interview or Duke. It seemed as if he attended the interview because his mother thought it was a good thing to do."

"On a scale from 1-10, David is a 5. I did not really click with this candidate. He seemed smart, yet a little cagey. Of the four people I have interviewed to date, I would rank him fourth. He struck me as someone who for Duke I would not recommend. He showed very little sign of passion. In fact, I started thinking during the interview that he may have a quietly cynical side."

Chuck comes bounding into my office, waving an application. "What's up, dude?"

"I found a mini-me!" He's very excited.

"What are you talking about?" He amuses me, and I'm glad to be taken away from reading these alumni interview reports.

"This young man, Rupal Patel, from Owensboro, Kentucky, is just like me when I applied to Duke six years ago! And not only that, he wrote his essay on the same topic that I did! You gotta read this, Rachel, it's great!"

"Hand it over," I say, grabbing for the file.

I shuffle through it. Rupal is a 55534 with a 5 in testing. He's a valedictorian whose teachers like his intellect but love his character. They gush over his compassion and respect for his classmates, say he's a real leader in the school. He's president of the student council and on the regional champs tennis team. His main interest is in chemistry; he and his teacher traveled around the state showing public school teachers how to use microchemistry in their classrooms. Rupal also taught a chemistry honors section in a local middle school. He won numerous state and national awards, including a Wendy's Heisman Trophy for the state of Kentucky. He was also an extra in the movie *The Natural*.

I read his long essay:

"Last summer, I was fortunate enough to attend the Governor's Scholars Program (GSP), a six week academic program for high schoolers in the state of Kentucky. I say fortunate only now, for it was an awesome experience, but at this time last year, I was extremely hesitant about attending. Looking back, I realize the extent of my growth due to the program, both during my 6 weeks in Frankfort and throughout the five months I spent preparing for it. Over that period of time, my feelings for GSP progressed from those of apprehension and doubt to affection and appreciation. I wish that everyone could have an experience like the one I had there, for it will continue to affect me for years to come and will always hold a special place in my heart."

The essay went on to describe, in minute detail, the application process for Governor's school, the homesickness that came when he arrived at the school, and then gave an account of daily life at the summer school:

"Each week, when I attended my seminar group (a discussion group dealing with the problems of contemporary society), I contributed as much as possible to the conversation. I tried to look at an issue from all angles so as to attain the most from the discussions. I learned to respect other people's views and opinions, even though they are different from mine. I learned that people's backgrounds influence their beliefs. When I entered the program, I had incorrectly assumed that the majority of the people at GSP would be from modern towns and would, thus, hold relatively the same views as I do. This assumption, though, was far from reality. Some grew up in very small, rural areas, while others came from large cities with large city problems. I now understood better why people act in certain ways, think certain thoughts, and hold certain prejudices. Some people may never have been exposed to any ideas different from the ones in which they believe. I had definitely changed.

At the end of the six weeks, that once little voice was now singing loud and clear. I loved GSP, but it had to come to an end. I was heavy-hearted, for I had gone through a radical transforma-

tion with three hundred other scholars and had become insepara-
ble friends with some of them. I had learned to take chances, to
love learning, and to build a small community inside the bounds
of a harsh outside world. I did not want to leave it all and return
home. At the start, I did not want to go; yet at the finish, I did not
want to leave. I had undergone a change and experienced a program that I will never forget."

"Chuck, my darling," I say after I've finished reading. "Clearly
this is a wonderful young man, and clearly he should be admitted.
But—and I hate to tell you this—his essay is nowhere near great.
It's a perfectly solid three. Maybe a three plus. That's it. And, he
spelled Nietzsche wrong."

"Well, yeah, that's what I gave it. Really? How do you spell Nietzsche? But I do just love this kid."

"We all like people just like us," I say, and go back to reading my
alumni interview reports.

"Daniel is obviously very bright and articulate. Though still
somewhat unsure of his final academic plans, he currently is leaning towards Engineering as a field. I was left unconvinced of
Daniel's overall commitment to Duke, and whether he sees something special about Duke that resonates with him. Though he is
clearly intelligent and well spoken, I did not come away with a particular sense of uniqueness. Hence, I evaluate him as 'solid.' "

"While I did not actually interview Jessica, her handling of the
interview process gave me serious concern regarding her application to Duke. When she first returned my call, she would not leave
a phone number, forcing me to get back into my email and get her
number again. When I returned her call, I was only able to leave

another message. She waited over five days to return my call. We set up an interview for last Saturday. She called Friday night to say she could not keep the appointment because she had forgotten that she had to baby-sit. We reschedule for tonight. She called less than two hours before her appointed time and left a message that she had forgotten another commitment."

Jessica, as it turns out, was a double eight hundred who had withdrawn her application after having, no doubt, been admitted to another school.

None of these reports will be of much help in making admissions decisions. The most enthusiastic and personable interviewees are often and unfortunately academically weak. The kids that alumni find too geeky for Duke, well, those tend to be the ones whose applications I love. These interview reports grew out of hours of anxiety on the part of applicants, and a not trivial amount of work on the part of the alumni. But to me, in terms of reading the applications, they are essentially useless—as are, generally, the interview reports written by admissions officers.

Those students able to come to campus to take the tour, who had arranged in advance an interview with an admissions staff member, were, by and large, not our strongest applicants. I hated being assigned the in-house duty of interviewing. Meeting with four or five kids a day, I quickly lost energy. The interviews were scheduled to last thirty minutes; I was usually able to get them in and out in twenty, flat. Though the kids tended to be well spoken and well bred, most of them were dull. Occasionally I met a great kid, and in that case, I'd not only write up the interview, I'd take care to try and print them neatly.

I shuffle through the tall pile of alumni interview reports and pull out the ones rated either five or one. The great mass in the middle, all those solid threes are simply not worth filing in the applications. The reason to try to file the fives and the ones is to be on the alert if the selection committee doesn't agree with the alum: if we deny a kid that they think is the best they've ever interviewed, it's good to be prepared for the inevitable huffy phone call with a list of reasons why (it helps if she doesn't have good grades or if testing is way below average). Likewise, if we admit a kid that they think was surly, untidy, or too geeky for Duke and that kid shows up at a party for accepted students, these alumni can get pretty steamed.

The interviews are well intentioned on both sides. Applicants try to present themselves as best they can; interviewers try to write up their impressions in a way that they think will be helpful. Sometimes they are. But as is typical of the whole process of applying to highly selective schools, what's hard is that there are so many applicants and they all look so so much alike.

Selection committee rounds are in two weeks. That means all applications must be read, all auto decisions must have been put through so that they can be entered into the system. Of course, each day the first readers bring back more applications for us to read. One first reader, hired on new this year, got so far behind in the reading that she decided to quit. But she never told anyone, and she didn't bring back the files. Finally the associate in charge of dealing with first readers had to threaten to send the police after her if she didn't return the two dozen applications in her possession. She dropped them off at the front desk and slunk away.

I have been able to run off preliminary reports, the most important of which is the "school group overview," the SGO. This lists all applicants by school in zip code order by state. It shows the high school zip code, the ETS code, the high school name, the last name of the applicant, the college (arts and sciences or engineering), race, decision, reason, rank in class and class size, GPA, SAT verbal, SAT math, ACT, reader-rating sum, and the ratings from the first reader and the admissions officer. This is a handy tool for preparation and also to take on the road so that you can look quickly, just before you visit a school, and find out what happened last year. Eight kids applied, you took the valedictorian and an athlete, but denied everyone else, including a kid with a perfect 1600. The "slate" is the official document used in decision rounds. It is similar to the SGO. Reading across, you have application number, full name of the applicant (last, first, middle), school, sex, race, applying for financial aid (we note this, but do not "see" it), alum, rank/size, GPA, SATs and SAT IIs, reader ratings (from both readers), sum, supplemental materials rating, interview rating, alum, dev, decision, reason.

Even at this point, with two weeks to go before rounds, there are plenty of decisions recorded. All of the kids that I put through as auto denies appear on the SGO as RZ (regular deny) and the reason is DIR (director). The same is true for my auto admits; they show up as RA (regular admit) with the same decision reason, DIR. Then there are the RW, the kids who have already withdrawn their applications. These are heartbreaking: they are often the strongest applicants, the kids you are most excited about. They have gotten in early to another school.

The only other kids who show up with decisions are those I've never heard of: the athletes. Their process is different, and for most recruited athletes, I never even see their applications. The senior associate is the liaison to the athletic department. Coaches bring her the transcripts and test scores of the kids they have already identified as athletes they want to recruit. She either gives them the OK to go ahead or she tells them to forget it. She reads the applications when they come in and, single-handedly, makes the admissions decision. All of a sudden you're looking at your school group, and there, usually toward the bottom of the list (they are listed in descending GPA order), is an applicant you've never heard of, who has already been admitted.

Looking over my SGO I get an idea of how many more applications I have to read: those with no reader ratings entered. There are a number of them. It is my responsibility to track them down and make sure I have read them before rounds. If the first readers haven't seen them, I have the option of reading them solo and doubling my ratings. I prefer not to do this, as it seems more fair to have an application read by at least two people; if I put them through as an auto deny, I will be making the decision on my own. I like having another person's impression of the applicant. Also, I am notoriously bad at certain kinds of details: I rely on the first readers to pick up things I might miss.

I have been reading diligently over the past month and a half and have never had a big backlog of applications. Having been an editor, charged with reading five-hundred-page manuscripts on scholarly subjects, I am unintimidated by the volume. This is less true for some of my colleagues, who have boxes of unread appli-

cations at home. They are starting to look haggard, these colleagues of mine. I wonder how astutely they will be reading in the
next couple of weeks.

I wonder about some of the applications I read at the end of
long days—were my ratings more generous, my readings more
careful, in the mornings? I know about myself that I am sharpest in
the morning; starting at around 11:00 A.M. I begin a mental
decline. By early evening I'm good for nothing. I spent many late
nights in these past few weeks reading applications.

As the deadline nears, I must place all of my applications—the
seven hundred or so that remain after the autos have been
processed—in alphabetical order, so that the secretary for my
"team" (a loose group of four admissions officers headed by an
associate) can "sweep" the files. This means going through and
looking in the "bed," or file in the filing room, for each applicant to
make sure that any new information gets into the folder, or
"jacket," that I have in my office. An application is considered complete when we have the part 1 (the name, address, and check); the
transcript; a counselor recommendation and one teacher rec; and
the part 5, the personal statement and extracurricular information. That means that after an application has been labeled complete and has been read, there may be the second teacher
recommendation, additional letters either from or on behalf of the
applicant, or other supplemental materials that have been sent in,
left in the bed. Since I've already made decisions on those who
were put through as autos, regardless of the additional material
lying fallow in their file room bed, and I've already read the applications of almost of all these kids, I just skim the recently added

letters. Sometimes the second teacher rec is vastly different from the first; mostly it confirms what you already knew. New test scores are supposed to be added automatically onto the slate—we get tapes from the ETS and download them directly into our system, so in most cases we don't have to worry about having the most recent scores.

It takes hours to alphabetize all these applications. It takes the secretaries forever to sweep. There's a sweeping schedule posted, and whole days are reserved for each team secretary to go through this process. These women work hard for their hourly wage.

After the files are swept and new stuff is added, I must put the newly alphabetized files into "slate order." This procedure takes far longer than alphabetizing. You have to follow the slate carefully. But you do get a nice overview of what is happening in each school. I could see at a glance that I had, for example, a total of sixteen applicants from Western High. Two were auto admits, one was an auto deny. There was also an athlete admitted behind my back. It was helpful to be able to see the dozen remaining files in one heap.

There were some schools where I had auto denied all three or four applicants. This is called, for some reason, "tubing the school." We don't like to tube our "feeder schools" but don't mind at all if it's a mediocre public high school somewhere. We do care about offending the guidance counselors at the fancy schools, who are in large part responsible for making up the "college lists" of the kids they advise. If they start steering applicants away, that can affect our numbers.

We wouldn't want to do anything to affect our numbers. Unless it's to make them go up.

Although counselors may actually counsel their students—giving them an honest appraisal of which schools were reaches, stretches, likely, and safety options—their stance toward admissions officers in the winter months was as lobbyists. I didn't quite realize this my first year until I was advised, by the woman who had read the New England schools before me, to set aside at least two full days to take "counselor calls."

It's a holdover, I think, from the days where the counselors of the best New England schools sat down with the admissions folks from Harvard, Princeton, and Yale to decide who would go where. It was a gentlemanly business, and everyone agreed on what made for a good Harvard man, a Yale man. Of course legacy status played a large role: the family has always attended Harvard. Done. Admit. Even if the young man was at the bottom of his class.

These counselors hold dear the belief that it is their right—not their privilege—to discuss their applicants with each school and to know of decisions before they are finalized. I learn the language: I go down my school group and tell the counselor "likely" for the students whom I know will be admitted, "possible," for those who will be placed on the waiting list, and "unlikely" for the ones I have already auto denied or am going to ask to be denied in rounds. Everybody understands this code, and most of the good counselors can predict the decision made by colleges.

At a handful of schools, I actually used the counselors to help me with the kids I wasn't sure about.

"He seems like a joiner to me," I said about one guy, perfectly fine but I couldn't find a reason to admit him.

"No," said Muffy from the Ezra Stiles School gently, "He's a glue guy. He keeps the class together."

She told me a story, about how there had been strife on the hockey team and how this young man had worked quietly behind the scenes to talk to the boys involved and get them to see the other side. Her story made me go back and read again, more carefully, the teacher recommendations and the kid's own writing. He had seemed nothing more than a solid academic student, but now, on rereading, signs emerged of an extraordinary character and a compassion, warmth, and maturity rare in a seventeen year old, especially one who had gone to an all-boys school all his life. I decided to argue in committee to have him admitted.

Many counselors simply wanted to know our decisions. Others affected shock when they heard them.

"I just cannot believe that you will not admit Binky. She is at the very top of the class," said Dana, the college counselor from the Jonathan Edwards School.

Earlier in the conversation she asked me what I was reading. I had received from her in December a copy of a well-reviewed but not particularly good book. It was inscribed, "To the most intellectual admissions officer I know." It struck me as rather strange at the time, but then, Dana had struck me as strange. It turned out that all of the admissions officers I met from other universities had stories about encounters with her.

"At the top of the class," I say. "How interesting."

There had been no way for me to glean that information from the school profile or from Dana's own letter. Her letter on behalf of Binky was similar to the letters she had written for the eight other applicants. They teemed with hyperbole and were filled with over-the-top, overwrought language: "exquisite poise," "delicious curiosity," "superlative swimmer," "joie-de-vivre," "je ne sais quoi."

Binky, with her ninety-two average, her four AP courses, her 680 verbal, 660 math testing, her two varsity field hockey letters, her tour guide pin, and her stilted and uninsightful meditation on a community service trip to Mexico, is their best student this year.

"I'm sorry, Dana," I say. "But it's unlikely that we'll be taking Binky, or any of the other kids this year. It was a very strong applicant pool. . . ."

As my voice trails off I hear a click, and then a dial tone.

Two days later I get an e-mail from the director: "Would you stop by my office at 3:00 P.M. on Wednesday? Got a call from Dana at Jonathan Edwards and want to discuss."

I come in ready to fight, prepared to defend my reasons for not wanting to admit any of their stinky students.

"Tell me about the kids," he says. "Are you sure there's no one you want to admit from this school group?"

"Not one."

"How about a courtesy waitlist for this Binky that Dana thinks is so great?"

I give him the rundown on her application. "She doesn't deserve to be placed on the waiting list, even if it would get Dana off our backs. She's not a strong enough applicant."

"Okay," he says. "Thanks. I'll call Dana back and tell her that if she has further questions, she should address them directly to you."

I found out later, from colleagues at Yale, Harvard, Georgetown, Penn, and Cornell, that it was Dana's modus operandi to call the deans of admissions when she wasn't happy with the news she received from an admissions officer. I guessed that I was no longer her favorite "intellectual."

I also receive a handful of calls from people wanting to know if there was anything in little Joey's application that needed clarification, was there anything missing?

"Are you Joey's dad?"

"Er, no. I'm his counselor."

"His high school guidance counselor? What happened to Joanne? I thought she was the counselor at Northside High?"

"Oh, well," he mutters. "I'm an independent college counselor, working with Joey on his applications."

Usually they were canny enough not to call, but I suppose since anyone can call himself a college counselor, and charge whatever people will pay, there were lots of newbies in the business who hadn't figured out how low they rank on the evolutionary scale.

I could often tell, when reading the application of a student, if she had received a lot of outside help. The polish on the applications would make them them appear slippery. On a number of occasions I simply did not believe that the essay had been written by the applicant. Most teachers will comment on a student's writing ability. If I received a beautifully written essay in a style that didn't jibe with the teacher's recommendation, I would be skeptical about who had written it. With so many qualified applicants, all they need do is give us one small reason to doubt them and we'll just pick someone else. Consultants may be able to control some parts of the process. What they can't control is the teacher's recommendations or how the student performs in class.

Our policy with the independent college counselors who called was to let them talk, but not to respond if they wanted to discuss the applicant. I always noted which applicants had had that additional help. It didn't help their applications. Other schools simply refused to take their phone calls. The services of these helping people are widespread, so much so that they are even being franchised. Kaplan Educational Centers and the Princeton Review are offering college admissions services. I wonder who's staffing? I know, from personal experience, how they hire their "teachers" for the test-prep courses. You are hired if you score high enough on the test you would like to teach. I taught both SAT- and MCAT-prep classes for Kaplan.

If you're not into the McDonald's approach, and you have the money, you go to an "independent college counselor" like the gentleman working with young Joey. A woman who had worked in admissions at Dartmouth for four years wrote a book about how to get into college and then set herself up as an independent counselor; she has a Web site offering her services:

A. Essay Review
(includes brainstorming session and as many revisions as necessary)
$1,500

B. Completion of Early Decision Application
(includes all parts of the application plus all essays)
$4,500

C. Completion of Other Applications After "B"

(assumes that B was already done)

$1,500 for first and $500 thereafter up to 8.

D. Completion of Regular Decision Applications

$4,500 and $500 thereafter up to 8.

E. Strategies for Transfer students applying to top schools

including 3 completed applications

$5,000 ($500 for each application over the third one)

The Four Year Complete High School Package

Includes everything listed in all the packages above from freshman (or 7th–8th grade for no extra charge to help course selection) year until all applications are completed. An A–Z guide to admissions including all applications necessary.

Her Web site no longer gives the sticker price for the four-year package. Soon after she posted it, the admissions community went ballistic: she was charging just under thirty thousand dollars for her soup-to-nuts package.

There are plenty of less expensive independent counselors out there. Some of them may even have worked in the admissions office of an elite college. Others, however, may say that they worked for Yale, but when pressed by someone who knows, it turns out that they were nothing more than first readers.

Parents are turning to these people in droves. I was talking to a friend, a New York publisher, who was deep in admissions angst on behalf of his daughter. I sat down with him and went over all the things I thought might be helpful for him to know. He thanked me, and then said that they were going to have a second meeting with the independent college counselor they'd hired.

"What do you know about her credentials," I asked.

"Well, nothing really, but everyone seems to like her."

"Why are you going to use her? I can answer all of the questions for you, and I'll do it for free."

"Oh," he said, "I guess it's just fear. I'm afraid that we'll somehow be left behind, that if everyone else is using her, we should as well."

7

The Emperor of Ice Cream: *Selection Committee Rounds*

I am troubled, troubled about love. Specifically, I'm worried about the ways in which we have been messed up by ancient and tenacious myths about romantic love.

Think of Plato's *Symposium*. A bunch of guys sit around drinking and talking. When it's Aristophanes' turn to give a speech in praise of love, he's already hiccuping from too much vino, and he fears that the others will laugh at him.

What he says is, in fact, pretty silly.

According to Plato's comic poet, humans were originally little round blobs, with four hands, four feet, and one head with two faces looking in opposite directions. They could walk, but when they really needed to move, they rolled.

At a certain point these roly-polies got uppity and tried to launch an attack on the gods. The gods were not pleased. Mighty Zeus decided to put the blobby critters in their place. So he smote them in two. Split, right down the middle.

Humans were ever after condemned to search the earth, looking for their lost "other half."

The notion that originally we were whole, and that the desire and pursuit of the whole is called love, is a whole lot of hooey. The idea of looking for someone else to complete you, whose identity can merge with your own, is pernicious. Aristophanes' joke is on us, because we keep buying into it. "You complete me," Tom Cruise says to his love interest in *Jerry Maguire*. "Mini-Me, you complete me," echoes Dr. Evil in *Austin Powers*.

There is another even more noxious myth: that romantic love has the power to transform and transfigure. Think of *Beauty and the Beast*.

Beauty is imprisoned by a monster. Through the power of her love she is able to turn him into something else. A prince. We see this all the time, good women with creeps. If only I love him enough, he will change. People change in fairy tales. Life, friends, is not so simple.

While it is often women who do such creative envisioning, men do it as well. Think about *Pygmalion*, or *Pretty Woman*. If you are a strong and powerful man, you can hector, harangue, and abuse anyone—a guttersnipe or a hooker—to become a suitable partner.

The most romantic present I ever got was a stapler. I was taking a bunch of classes while working as an editor and was constantly running to my office to staple my papers. I didn't have a stapler at home; just took it for granted that I'd have to drive three or four miles for a staple.

Mike, my physicist boyfriend, thought hard about how to fete me one Valentine's Day. He decided that a stapler would improve the quality of my life. He combined that gift with a pair of earrings he made out of electronic components found in his lab. My heart went pitter-pat.

Love is about seeing and being seen. To love someone is to see that person clearly and completely. To see their strengths and to see, too, their faults and weaknesses—and to love them still. You see what is there and understand and accept what is not. You do not expect them to complete you, nor do you want to change them. The best you can do, in my opinion, is to hope that someone will see you well enough to give you something that makes your life just a little better. Even if it is only a stapler.

Valentine's Day has come and gone. Now, in the first week of March, red hearts and roses have been replaced by Easter candy. My beloved little yellow Peeps have made their annual reappearance, and I think longingly of my aborted book project.

But book projects and dating and dinners with friends have all taken a backseat to the denouement of application reading: selection committee rounds.

"Come on, come on, come on. Whaddya got for me? Where are we, anyway?"

We've just returned from an hour-long lunch break. We've been at it since 8:00 A.M., and it's now just past two. The director's blood-sugar level seems to be back up.

I was delighted to be placed on Audrey's committee. She is a pro: an astute reader, a clear and concise presenter. The committee consists of two admissions officers, in this case myself and Missy, and the director. The rule is you have to feed your committee while you are presenting your slate of applicants. It's difficult, because it comes at a time when you're too busy to wash your hair, let alone think about cooking. It's also hard because of the director and his vexed relationship to food. Constantly on a diet, the man has a fierce sweet tooth. So the trick is to find food that he will enjoy and at the same time inspire the least amount of guilt and complaints about calories and fat grams.

Audrey is as good at this part of the job as she is at reading and presenting. She spent last night baking while trying to finish reading the last of her apps. She made sure to have the right combination of sweet (brownies, lemon bars, chocolate chip cookies) and savory (Camembert-stuffed mushrooms, smoked salmon on pumpernickel), along with some healthy stuff like carrots and grapes that no one has touched. As weariness sets in and blood-sugar levels begin to drop, decisions are not as judiciously made. Having food does help somewhat, but I always pitied the kids whose high schools came at the end of a long slate.

"Where are we? Colorado, right? Let's go. Into the mountains—heigh ho."

The director's energy level has clearly picked up. Before we broke for lunch he merely grunted assent or growled questions. Now he was positively frisky.

"Okay, here we go," says the director, leaning over to reach a lemon bar and pick up the first application on the pile that ascended from the floor. "Nicholas Anderer from Redwood High School. Let's hear about Mr. Anderer. Is he a wanderer? A panderer? A philanderer?"

"You're gonna love him," says Audrey.

166

"You think so? Well let's hear something about him first."

"Redwood High School, Redwood, Colorado. Ninety-two in the graduating class, twenty-two percent to two- and four-year colleges. Nick Anderer. We've got ourselves a rural val." Rural valedictorians are a hot commodity around selection-committee tables.

"Ah, a rural val." There was a general appreciative murmur from the committee.

"All honors classes, no APs even offered at the school, he's maxed out the curriculum. Never got below an A-, and he only got one . . . in ninth grade. He's clearly better than the school. The teachers don't know what to do with him. 'Best I've taught in thirty years.' 'I feel like he's the teacher and I'm the student.' Does no extracurriculars because he works on the family cattle ranch. He brain tans, as well."

Audrey says it matter-of-factly. Brain tans.

"Okay," I say, "I give. What's brain tanning?"

She was smug. She'd clearly learned this only very recently but was lording her newfound knowledge over the rest of us. "Far as I can tell, you kill the deer and then tan its hide using—yep, you guessed it—its own brain." She dangled a small, delicate leather pouch in front of us. "Sent in this sample of his work. It's really quite beautiful, I think."

"Gross," groans Missy.

"Brain tanning," says the director. "I like it. Almost—just almost—enough to overlook the extremely modest testing."

Poor Nick was coming in with a 1320. Far below what was acceptable.

"One more thing," adds Audrey. "First-generation college. And his mother is from Mexico. He's Latino."

"Admit," intones the director. "Next."

"Now we're at St. Ignatius College Prep in Golden. We have twelve apps from this all-boys school, and I'm recommending that we zip the school group."

"Deny the whole group? We can't find one admissible nice Catholic boy? What's the deal here?" The director says, grabbing another lemon bar and looking around for his ever-present coffee cup.

"We have an overzealous alum on the faculty at this school. She tells them all to apply. Then she gets pissed because we never take them. Sure, they would have gotten in when she was applying, but now they're just not competitive. Even as her Duke degree has become more valuable with our greater selectivity, she still wants it to be the same school it was twenty-five years ago."

"Not even one?" Missy asks. "How about this kid with the 1540 boards? Second in the class? Let's hear about him."

Blond Missy was always perky, except when she was being officious. While it was Audrey's job to represent the kids and argue for their admission, it was the committee who made the decision.

"Bruce Anthony Brewer. Goes by Brant. Nice testing, all As, except for a B in sophomore Spanish, taken a total of seven APs. President of the student body, captain of the baseball team, started a community service project to send books to a library in El Salvador. With the help, of course, of his wealthy family."

"Hey, he's sounding like an admit to me," says Missy.

"Jerk," Audrey answers.

"Pardon?" Missy is shocked to her dark brown Midwestern roots.

"The kid's a jerk. We don't want him."

"Say more." The director has stopped chewing and is now paying attention.

"His teachers agree that he's smart, very smart. But they also say the same thing. That he's not a nice person. No respect for others, especially those not as quick as he. And on a Post-it note attached to his guidance counselor recommendation came a little story. It's of course not part of his official record, but it seems he was accused of date rape by a girl from St. Benedicts, the sister school. His father's a judge in town. No charges were ever pressed."

"Deny. This we don't need." The director handed the file over to me. My job, in addition to sitting on the committee, is to stamp each file, either A for "admit," Z for "deny"—no one knows why—or L for "waitlist."

Audrey moves professionally through her slate, giving us the information we need whenever there is a question. She is confident in her recommendations, and they all make sense.

Then she gets to Central High School. She wants to admit the valedictorian and waitlist the number three in the class.

"Stop," I said.

She looked up at me, smiling.

"Connie Lutz—isn't she the one? . . ."

"Yes," she said, "she is."

Audrey had come to me a few weeks ago to discuss an application. Connie Lutz's record was good, but not stellar. She had taken hard classes and done well enough, but her testing was a little soft and her teachers' endorsements were typically enthusiastic but not over the top. She hadn't seemed to have done much in high school.

What Audrey wanted to show me was her required explanation of a disciplinary action taken against her junior year. I read it. I asked to see her other essays. I fell in love with Connie Lutz.

"Do you have an opinion on this applicant, Rachel?" the director asks.

"I do. I think we should admit her."

"Oh really," he says. "I'm looking at a string of fours here, and Audrey is suggesting we waitlist young Connie. What do you know about her application that makes you think she should be admitted?"

"She was suspended junior year. Why don't you read to the committee her explanation of the disciplinary action against her?"

"Audrey?"

"Well," Audrey says, "I'd love to admit her, but I didn't think you'd go for her. Maybe you should go ahead and read the statement."

He riffled through the folder and found the attached explanation, a single sheet of paper with the heading "Disciplinary Action." He reads aloud:

"I wouldn't take it back. I wouldn't exchange those minutes I spent sitting red faced in the office in front of my assistant principal, not even for an unstained permanent record, one I wouldn't have to explain. The blemish was not to be escaped, but it was better suited to paper than my conscience. Given a chance, I'd relive the phone call to my parents, that horrible aching feeling, and the interview with Officer Hernandez. I'd relive the questions of a nosy reporter and the front-page story in the local paper. I wouldn't make the same mistake again, but I wouldn't erase the one I made.

"I had never been in her office before. I sat there looking at Ms. Boyd in her pink suit. She repeated her question. 'Did you eat a marijuana brownie today on the field trip?' My heart raced. Her eyes almost smiled through her thick glasses as she waited for my denial. I desperately wanted to tell her that no, I hadn't done such a thing, and slip out of that suffocating room unscathed. The girls before me had done just that. How simple . . . I would just lie and keep my shame to myself. They very thought of returning to Mr. Snyderman's front row seat in physics made me shudder. He would hate me.

"She waited, eyebrows raised. I wasn't worried about what my parents would say. They knew me and trusted me. Eating pot-laced brownies was not among my habitual activities. My teachers though . . . Ms. Jackson . . . Ms. Levi . . . Mr. Tuttle . . . God help me . . . Mr. Tuttle. I began to realize the enormity of my mistake. My mouth had all but formed my lie when I said, 'Yes.' I said it again. 'Yes. I had one.'

"What followed was of little significance. I was suspended, among other things. I served my one-day sentence and returned to school. If everyone hated me, they hid it well. Everything was surprisingly as it had been. I didn't hang my head quite as low as I had expected.

"I was embarrassed at my lapse in judgment, yes. I didn't look Mr. Snyderman in the eye for a month. However, as those weeks in May passed, I became increasingly at ease with my new delinquency. I looked at my friends, some of whom had cheated their way to a spotless record of conduct. I didn't envy them in the least. I made a mistake and I was owning up to it. It took me a while to realize that all it made me was . . . human. Not evil. Not stupid. Not crazy . . . just human.

"I made the necessary apologies and completed my required counseling. I marched down to the local newspaper after they ran their ill-advised story and gave them a piece of my 17 year old mind. I eventually stopped feeling like such a bad kid and came to realize that the very situation, which I had expected to ruin my junior year, only forced me to grow and take responsibility—to be honest with myself.

"I wish I could report that I was suspended for chaining myself to a cafeteria table to make a statement about civil liberties. Actually, I wish I didn't have to report anything at all. However, the fact is that I made a mistake, a big one, on a bright May afternoon at a theme park, in a temporary epidemic of teenage stupidity.

"Never would I have imagined that my decision would teach me so much; more than I could ever |have| hoped to learn otherwise on a physics field trip. I learned about the bigger roller coaster that we all ride—life."

"Wow," says the director.

"Yes," I say. "Wow. Her other essays are even better."

"Look," I say, "her testing stinks. And she's not a joiner, she's a thinker. She's also a darn good writer."

"Rachel," says the director. "I've told you before, we don't ever say testing 'stinks.' We say her testing is modest."

"Excuse me," I know I should know better. I know I should try harder. "Her testing is modest."

"What do you want to do with her, Audrey?"

"I'd love to take her."

"Missy," he asks, "what do you think?"

"I think Rachel just likes her because she herself probably got caught eating a pot brownie in high school."

"Never got caught. And to tell the truth, I don't think that at age seventeen I wrote as well as she does."

"Missy," the director says, "I'm leaning toward taking her. Are you okay with that?"

She twirls her hair around a nail-polished finger.

"I suppose so." Reluctant, grudging.

"Okay, let's take her."

We are coming to the end of Colorado. There were some cool kids, outdoorsy types who had bagged the big peaks, skied the black diamond trails, rafted the wily rivers. And lots and lots of mountain bikers. Audrey loved those kids, and we let her have a number of them. We took a bunch of valedictorians and denied a number of them as well. Also denied some boring kids with great testing. The director hated to do that—he loved being able to boost the median reported SAT.

"Next school is Boulder Creek. I gotta tell you about Jessie Hunt. When I visited the school, she came into the room trailing her dad. Apparently they had a friendly disagreement about which was more stressful, school or work. So Jessie asked him to accompany her to school for the day. They had just taken a calculus test before coming to hear me talk about Duke. She explained why her dad was with her. I asked how the calculus test went for him. Told me that he had gone to MIT some years ago; too many to remember much calculus. Jessie asked thoughtful questions and even invited me to come to the rehearsal of the play she was directing. I'm recommending admit."

There was stunned silence. We were all looking down at our slates. While Jessie's grades and scores were fine, they certainly didn't measure up to the standards of admitted students. She had mostly fours, with a couple of threes.

The director finally speaks up. "What do her teachers say?"

"Well," Audrey hesitates, "the Ds. Dedicated, determined, diligent. And a really good person," she adds in a whisper.

"What does she do outside of class?" I ask, hoping to help Audrey out. She clearly wanted this kid in.

"She does theater, is on the cross-country and soccer teams, though only JV. NHS, Amnesty International—she wrote her essay about seeing the Dalai Lama at the Peace Jam in Denver."

Audrey was flailing.

"Audrey, let me ask you a question," the director said gently. "If you hadn't met Jessie and her dad, would you be arguing to admit her?"

She took a breath before she answered. "You're right. She's a typical BWRK. I just liked her."

"We're not saying she can't go to college," the director said, reaching for a brownie. "We're just saying it's not gonna be Duke. Next."

Upstairs, there is a concomitant selection committee meeting going on, being chaired by the senior associate. She has been in admissions for over a decade and is a good and earnest person, not unsmart. But she is more conservative than the director. She waxes sentimental and focuses on the minutiae of grades and testing and class rank rather than looking for signs of less orthodox but more intellectual life. The decisions she makes on kids are often different from the ones the director would have made on the same applications. She likes students who write sappy essays about their mothers. She brings warmth to the office and talks incessantly about her favorite kids. She remembers all of them. She is a lovely person, and I fear ever having her chair my selection committee rounds. She believes in the value of hard work, and tends to like the pluggers who got the job done, without flare or panache.

During breaks in selection rounds, admissions officers not presenting or on committee would pop in to see how things were going or to graze off the food. We gossiped about any interesting kids. Victoria was dying to tell me the story of what had happened in a committee she served on. Apparently, there was a math genius kid, double eight hundreds, top of his class, teacher recs said that he could walk on water. He had gone to the International Math Olympiad, a rare honor. He wrote his book essay on *Anna Karenina*. Not unusual. He wrote, however, that at the same time he was reading about cuckoldry, he was experiencing it. His girlfriend began cheating on him: "One day she was hanging out with my best friend, the next day she was giving him blow jobs." One of the admission officers was horrified. She didn't want to admit him. The committee managed to make her see that her position was too rigid. Victoria argued that the kid was probably going to go to MIT anyway, and that he was just testing us, to see what we would do. Over the objections, the committee prevailed and "the blow job guy" as we came to refer to him, was admitted.

Sitting in on rounds is fascinating. It's the only time you get a real overview of the process. You see each regional officer present his or her region, and what you realize is that, perhaps obviously but also strikingly, there are huge regional differences. We would attract the best students from Florida. You'd see enormous school groups, with the top fifteen students in a class applying. Virginia was another state with very strong applicants. Having secured a reputation as an excellent school in the South, it was easy for Duke to attract the applications of the best students of the South. Chuck, the admissions officer who read applications from Kentucky, Tennessee, Oklahoma, Arkansas, Indiana, and Pennsylvania— always had amazing applicants that he would talk about at length, both in and out of committee. They were amazing both because many of the top kids in some of these states were not applying to Harvard, Yale, and Princeton but rather to Duke, Emory, and the

University of Virginia, and also because Chuck was such a close and astute reader of their applications.

When I first met him, I hated Chuck. He seemed a typical Duke BWRK. I remember his saying when we both started working in admissions that he could talk about college basketball for hours. He wasn't kidding. When we had a reader-training session and were asked to evaluate sample applications and share our opinions, he said, about a very mediocre essay, "Well, I think it's good because I'm not a very good writer and this is better than anything I could have come up with."

Chuck turned out to be not only one of my favorite admissions officers but one of my favorite people in the world. In many ways, he is a typical Dukie. Especially in the sense that the casual surface belies an interior that is rich, deep, and complex. He has an open and exacting mind and a rare generosity of spirit. This made him a wonderful advocate. Though he never became a great reader of personal essays, giving most kids threes, even when they wrote, by my lights, five-quality stuff, he was a most astute reader of recommendations. He paid incredible attention to detail and was able to pick up small things that made a huge difference.

He was also the most solid of citizens within the office. His computer skills combined with a workaholic personality to keep him late most nights, working on the Web site (not his job), creating reports and statistical analyses (not his job), going into the AskDuke account and answering backlogs of hundreds of E-mails (not his job), doing favors for the director (everyone's job), and doing all of these things well and happily.

I loved sitting in on his rounds because he knew all of his kids so well, and he wanted to talk about each and every one of them in detail (he did have a habit of going on a bit too long, but it was as endearing as it was exasperating). He would spend as much time talking about the kids who were clear denies as he would about those he was most excited about having admitted. He was smart as all get-out, hardworking, earnest, and good.

He lasted two years as an admissions officer and then took a job in computer consulting.

The admissions officer who read New Jersey would complain bitterly about how similar all her kids were—high testing, hard curricula, good grades, the same old extracurriculars—it was difficult to tell them apart; the Midwest representative always feared having me on her committee because she thought that I would think that all her kids were boring; I used to joke about Florida—you could send your worst recruiter to that state and still get loads of applications, unlike my difficult task of recruiting in New England, trying to get them out of the jaws of the Ivy League. Texas, we all know, is not part of the United States. The person who read Texas appreciated those larger-than-life Texans, and they loved her for it. Most of us loved our kids and felt closely tied to our regions.

There was something else, too, that made this time of year feel different. The director was inaccessible to his staff most of time. He led the weekly staff meetings, then disappeared behind a door that was always closed. He rarely made it to the second floor of the building, where most of us had our offices. But during rounds, admissions staff were finally able to spend time with him. The director was kind of like a seafaring dad, always away, and for the brief moment when he was home, magnanimous and available. At the same time, he was mercurial. Subject to fits of pique and worse. Unwilling to accept less than total preparedness. If the parts of the application were out of order (which they often were, since people were always pawing through them to find stuff), he would severely admonish the presenter. If something had been missed, especially if it was something he thought important, he would chastise. So the staff greeted rounds, especially when the director chaired their committee, with a mixture of excitement and trepidation.

I knew that since I am bad at details, generally sloppy, and don't care as much as I know I should, I would likely be scolded for some minor transgression. As it turned out, that my folders were occasionally out of order became fodder for gentle teasing. That, and the horrid truth that no one, not even I, could read my handwriting.

In order to prepare for rounds, after you put all of the jackets in slate order, you have to go through every application and tear off the "yellow sheet." The reader-rating card is printed in triplicate, so that the top sheet is yellow, the next is green, and the bottom is a harder manila sheet. Each presenter will use her stack of yellow sheets in order to present applicants. The members of the committee will have a copy of the slate, which gives the reader ratings and other information, and the committee chair—either the director or the senior associate—will have the actual application. The idea, while reading, is to make sure that all the pertinent notes are on the yellow sheets—the more germane comments from the recs, your own notes on essays, the important extracurriculars, and the grade grid. The yellow sheet should be a snapshot of the student.

Audrey's yellow sheets were works of art. Her tiny, delicate, but incredibly neat handwriting filled almost every available space. As she prepared for rounds, she went back and underlined in different colors various points she wanted to make.

The director gave explicit instructions on how he wanted applicants presented during rounds. Start with your recommendation: I would like the committee to admit/deny/waitlist this applicant. Give a thumbnail description of why. If the committee wants to know more, move on to a greater level of detail, prepared, if necessary to go to yet another level.

Of course, it rarely happened this way. Nothing would annoy the director more than when an admissions officer started out by saying "I love this kid." But often, we couldn't help ourselves.

With big school groups, where large numbers of kids applied from the same high school, he'd want to know the history of what "we'd done" there last year. How many applicants and what the decisions were. If we'd tubed an important school, or taken the three top kids but none had matriculated, it could factor into this year's decisions. We might take a weaker student in the hopes of establishing a relationship with the school. There's nothing like having an enthusiastic first-year college student return to her high school in the fall, talking about how much she loves her university, to increase applications. For that reason, we took special care with decisions on kids who were clearly "impact" kids in their high school, where everyone in the school would be aware of their college application process and its outcome.

Preparing for rounds is laborious. Before you rip off the yellow sheet and take it out of the application, you have to make sure that it contains everything you think you might need. That means glancing again at the various parts of the application and trying to decipher what you have transcribed. Many of the admissions officers didn't finish reading until just before their rounds, and so they had little time left for "prep." This showed in committee. As did the fact that they'd read some of the applications later and therefore much less carefully than others. Dave's yellow sheets were notoriously blank. He read applications from a region that sent a large number of extremely talented students, with high testing and loads of AP courses in their curriculum selection. When asked, in committee, what a kid did extracurricularly his answer would invariably be "sports, clubs, music." He could give the topics of the essays, but nothing more. So the director would read the application while the committee sat and waited. After a cursory review, he would tell us what he had found interesting in the kid's application, and then the committee would make a less-than-well-informed decision.

There are also green sheets. They are the same reader-rating cards, the ones under the yellow sheets. But for applicants of color, the yellow sheets stay with the specific recruiters, and when you go into rounds you have your yellow sheets for the Caucasian applicants and green sheets for the students of color It's easy to see how diverse the pool is simply by looking at the stack of reader-rating cards. Mostly you see yellow.

There's one person responsible for African American applicants, another for Hispanic/Latino applicants. These recruiters get the applications after the first reader has read them. They do a second read and then pass them on to the regional officer, who reads them, fills in her two cents on the reader-rating card, and gives the yellow sheet back so that they have a record of all the applicants of color. This is meant as a safeguard. The assumption is that these recruiters will read with a sensitivity to race not present in the regional officers. They will pick up on salient facts that may be overlooked by the admissions officer and will have a better overall sense of the pool, comparing the students of color to each other rather than to the white applicants.

The Hispanic/Latino recruiter's job is complicated by having to decide when ethnicity or race should be considered. For example, do we give a boost to applicants of Spanish background more so than we would other European Americans? Are the Cuban Americans in Miami a traditionally oppressed minority in this country who need the extra push of Affirmative Action? If a student has a mother of Mexican origin and checks his race as "Latino" but has had no contact with Hispanic culture, does not know Spanish, and is a child of privilege, should he be considered with the white kids or the Latinos?

Duke was firmly committed to Affirmative Action. We took kids with far lower reader-rating sums if they were students of color. We knew the statistics about the way SATs tracked with family income: in a direct and parallel relation. There are a good number of great programs that send talented black students to private schools. At many of my Massachusetts prep schools I saw numbers of African Americans. My feeling was if they could do the work at these competitive high schools, they would be able to handle Duke. The auto admit parameters for African Americans were considerably lower, since the reader-rating sums were in general lower.

Admissions officers generally didn't know what to do with students of color. All sorts of confusion about race and class reared its ugly head in reading and selection committee meeting discussions. There was very little open talk about what the policy was about Affirmative Action and what the philosophical underpinnings were. Most of the admissions officers seemed not to understand essential arguments about why Duke was committed to the policy. With the admissions officers who were my friends I tried to discuss larger social and cultural issues relating to race, generally with the result of frustration on both sides. With the colleagues that I didn't like or respect, I rolled my eyes when they made racist comments or snapped harshly—and unproductively—at them. There were no intelligent counterarguments to the policy from the admissions officers, no serious naysayers working to undermine it. There was merely a tacit acceptance that the students of color would be somehow "weaker." The contact—if any—that most admissions officers had with current African American students was reduced to talking to, or simply listening to, the campus leaders, many of whom were middle-class male students, a minority of a minority. As in many other places, it was the African American women from less monied backgrounds who struggled to make things work out.

If left in the hands of admissions officers, the way Duke's rating system is set up, there would be very few students of color. Thus we have an African American recruiter. She would, after reading an application, decide if a student should be invited to BSAI, Black

Student Alliance Invitational (a weekend that happened in March), where the top applicants of color would be invited to campus, hosted by current students, and shown around. Current students were conflicted about BSAI. I heard from a number of them that when they came for the weekend as applicants, it looked to them that Duke was a place where they'd feel comfortable: all of black Duke came out for BSAI. There were step shows, fashion shows, parties, dances, black people everywhere. What they learned when they got to campus as students was that for the rest of the year, it was an overwhelmingly white school, a rich white school. When it was their turn to host prospective students during the weekend, many of them were painfully torn between wanting to recruit more students of color to the university and wanting to tell them the truth about what the school was like for African Americans.

I learned, by sitting on a committee on residential life for "independents"—those students who chose not to join a fraternity or selective house—how much the housing situation at Duke contributes to a sense of disempowerment on the part of students of color. Since none of the black fraternities are given housing on the main quad (where all of the white fraternities are located), the students of color must pay to rent space for their parties. They must also pay for "security." Most of the black student parties are alcohol free; most fraternity parties are drunken bashes. But the wealthy white kids didn't have to pay for security.

Students were invited to BSAI before they knew whether they would be admitted. Many felt that their admission would be contingent upon showing up, and so scraped together the money to get to campus, many of them taking long bus rides through the night. The weekend was filled with anxiety. They didn't want to love it too much because what if they didn't get in? Theoretically only students who would be admitted were supposed to be invited; in practice that was not the case. The director wanted to leave some wiggle room if any of these kids slacked off during their senior year in high school and their grades slipped. Though I knew that most of them would be admitted, they had no idea. I sat at a table at a BSAI dinner with seven great kids. I loved them, they were smart and funny and warm. But all they wanted to talk about were their chances of getting in. They would see each other again, as many of the top schools have similar weekends, both for African Americans and for Latinos.

In some idealized imagined future, there would be no need for a weekend like BSAI. Nor would there be a need for specific recruiters. One of my colleagues, years later, was still steamed about having to admit an African American young woman from rural Georgia whom she just didn't think deserved to be at Duke. She had argued passionately to deny her; her committee and the African American recruiter had overturned her. I had coincidentally gotten to know this young woman, who amazed me as much in our own private conversations as she did when I heard her speak up at a meeting of the Duke trustees. She taught a course on issues of feminism and domestic violence. She was writing an honors thesis comparing subversive women in *Middlemarch*, *To the Lighthouse*, and a handful of Toni Morrison novels.

If she didn't belong at Duke, I don't know who did.

8

Ivy Day in the Committee Room: *More Rounds*

I have been challenged. I received an E-mail from a dean of admissions at another school. He had read something I'd written for *The Chronicle of Higher Education* and invited me—challenged me—to contribute an essay to a column that he had helped to develop for the *Journal of College Admission*, the publications organ of the national association for college admissions. Deans at various schools had been asked to answer the questions they asked of their own applicants. The response to the call for submissions had been an embarrassing silence.

At first I said no. I'm not a dean. And I didn't want to write for no money.

Then I thought more about it. I didn't want to be like those deans, unwilling to expose themselves the way we expect—the way we demand—that our applicants do. So I agreed.

I decided to answer the Duke book question. Of course it was a bit contrived, since I'd read the book I chose to write about long ago. But, I figured, probably my best applicants would do the same thing.

I submitted my essay.

"I have been grappling with the luxuries of whiteness. It's not that I haven't thought about issues of race and privilege and power before; I have. Lots. But recently it became more personal, more intimate. Being a white heterosexual woman has afforded me the opportunity to be in control of my sexuality and of representations of it. Previously, when people passed me on the street kissing a boyfriend, they'd smile. Now it's not so simple.

"Being white means that I have a choice about when I want to think about race matters. And I've chosen to think a fair amount about them, but only when I want to. Dating an African American man changed that. It exposed me to salacious comments from black men on the street, to the enmity of African American women who have even a harder time than I finding a good man to date, to the obsequious pandering of liberal white people who go out of their way not to appear racist, and to rethinking some of my own assumptions. It's hard to give up the luxury of thinking about race only when I choose to.

"In fact I gave up not being able to think critically and carefully about race after reading Patricia Williams's *Alchemy of Race and Rights*. A law professor, she's brutally and touchingly incisive. 'The original vehicle for my interest in the intersection of commerce and the Constitution was my family history,' she writes. 'A few years ago, I came into the possession of what may have been the contract of sale for my great-great-grandmother.'

"Patricia Williams tells stories. Stories change lives. Her account of being locked out of a Benetton store in Soho on a Saturday afternoon by a white teenaged bubble-gum-chewing store clerk is breathtaking in both the power of its language and the fact that the story will not surprise many African Americans, while white folks respond by saying, 'That's unbelievable.' 'He snuffed my sense of humanitarian catholicity, and there was nothing I could do to snuff his, without making a spectacle of myself.'

"But she did make a spectacle of herself. The story, her telling of this story in this book and in this way, became an important moment in legal studies, in the movement called Critical Race Theory. The book shook me, moved me often to tears. I was more shaken though, by those who did not respond to it as I did. Those in and out of the academy who dismissed Williams as just another angry black woman.

"Telling the truth, it seems, just isn't good enough."

I was so resentful of being expected to cook for my committee during early decision rounds that I did not. Instead I brought in pretzels and a couple of bags of Tootsie Rolls. For this I was chastised. Later in the day, when I got as hungry and as crabby as the members of my committee, I realized what a huge tactical error it had been. Hungry crabby people (who are mad at you for not feeding them) are less likely to go along with your recommendations. A committee that experiences a mad sugar rush after scarfing down Tootsie Rolls and then crashes—it's not a pretty sight. I make sure to bring in good food for my regular decision rounds. Including a few boxes of Peeps.

Also, I have lucked out. The people who form my committee are my friends, Victoria and Chuck.

My slate starts in Massachusetts, by zip code. The first applicants I present are from western Massachusetts, representing a mixture of rural public high schools and some of the tonier boarding schools.

I start out by giving an overview. I've received a target of eighty admits and eighty waitlists from my entire region, which consists of both Massachusetts and northern California. While recruiting we say that we don't have quotas. This is technically true, though we do, at this point in the process, get regional targets. We want, of course, to be able to matriculate students from all fifty states. It is left up to me how I want to divide my admits, and I tell the committee that I am recommending thirty-eight admits from Massachusetts, thirty-nine from northern California. I have three Ao's. A subzeros are less enthusiastic admits. If at the end of my rounds there is space left, these are the kids who will be pulled in, just as if we are over—if the committee gets too enthusiastic about too many of my kids—they are the ones who will be pulled back. During rounds, we try not to keep an exact count, making decisions instead on the quality of the applicants we want to admit. Afterward, however, we must, as a committee, come in "on target." There are forty kids from each state that I am recommending a waitlist decision on.

I report the numbers from the big feeder schools, how they compare to last year's numbers. I give the committee the breakdown showing that applications are up in both of my states.

"Okay," says the director, pulling out the first application and looking at the slate. "It looks like you've already gotten rid of your first three schools." I had auto denied applicants at the first two and had auto admited a kid from the third.

"So here we are at Western Mass Regional High School with young Mr. Thomas Brown. What would you like to do with Mr. Brown?"

"*Tom Brown's School Days* were fine but nothing worth writing home about."

They don't get my pretentious little joke.

So I continue. "I am recommending waitlist for Tom. He's fourth in the class out of 332, but his curriculum wasn't that strong, four APs out of sixteen offered. Recs are good, but not outstanding, and he's flat on the end." At the end, the end of the reader ratings, were the evaluations of his essays and of his PQs/ECs—personal qualities and extracurriculars—he was a three in both categories. "His testing isn't bad, though."

"Not bad at all," says the director, looking at the slate and seeing 740 verbal, 780 math.

"Yeah, I know, but I have better kids with testing that's as good. Tom is a fine and upstanding young man, but nothing sparkles on his application."

As I am finishing this sentence the director has already signed the jacket and has passed it on to Chuck, the committee member responsible for stamping the decision, which will later be entered into the computer.

"Next is Nicola Bastion at West High School. I'm recommending deny."

"Done," says the director. Her ratings speak for themselves. She is 18 out of 309, 680/690, six APs, weak essays (according to my rating), and typical ECs.

"Hmm," says Victoria, the other member of my committee, "looks like this little Smith kid from the Sillimon School that you auto denied will be coming back."

We all look at the slate. Robert Smith had ratings of straight threes. Completely average in our pool. Not a chance of getting in, I had thought. But on the slate there appear two notations, marking him as a "coded" applicant. Under the alum rating he is listed as high. That means not only did he have a parent who had gone to Duke, but also that they had donated in the top percentile of giving. Just having an alum parent didn't help; they had to have a history of consistent giving in order to have legacy status kick in on the admissions front. But Rob Smith was a "high high." The development office had also coded him as one of their top draft picks for the year. High highs would come back through the alumni and development rounds that took place after the regular selection committees had met.

"That boy's gonna be getting in," says Chuck, one of whose in-office responsibilities was to prepare the slates for the alum and development committee rounds.

"Not through any efforts of mine," I reply.

"No kidding," says the director. "You are not supposed to be auto denying alumni kids."

"Oops," I say, sheepishly. "I guess I missed that when I read the application."

"Moving on," he says, "to the Calhoun School."

"Okay," I say, "here's the overview. We have thirty-nine applicants from this school, up from twenty-seven last year. Last year we took seven and enrolled three, two of which were development admits. This year we've already taken two early, and denied one. We also had an athletic admit. I recommend that we take another three here, waitlist seven, and deny the rest. Four of those I'm recommending deny on will come back, because they're coded. And if you look at some of those last names, you will see why they're coded."

The director issued a low whistle, recognizing American aristocracy when he saw it.

"Good. Tell us about the kids you want to admit."

I go through in slate order. The top two are clear admits, though we will take them and my sense is that they will turn us down and go to Harvard, Yale, or Princeton. Next on the slate are my waitlists. Then, toward the bottom, I come to Claire Hess, my anorexic tour guide.

"I want to take Claire," I say.

"You have got to be kidding," says Chuck, looking at her reader ratings. "She's got a three in achievement. And that's generous."

They all look at me.

Finally, the director says, "Okay, let's hear about her."

I tell them about her battle with anorexia, about what I have learned of her family situation from the counselor. I point to her testing, a combined 1520. I read portions of the teacher recs that I have transcribed onto my yellow sheet. She wrote her book essay on *Pride and Prejudice*, I point out, throwing a bone to Victoria, whose predilection for nineteenth-century literature is well known. Finally, I ask the director to read aloud the first few sentences of her long essay for the committee.

He does.

There is silence.

"Look," I say, "she can do the work. She's smart, she's insightful. She's going to get into Yale; we may not even get her. But I think, on her merits, she deserves to be admitted."

"But don't you think," Victoria asks, "that her eating disorder will put her at risk here?"

"She's going to carry that around with her wherever she goes. And it's frankly not our business to evaluate her on her illness. It's the insight into it that's important. She's a brave young woman. I want to take her."

"What do you guys think?" the director asks the committee.

Chuck shakes his head.

"Don't get me wrong," he starts off. "I think she's had a hard time. But are we rewarding her for being anorexic? I mean, would we take anyone else with these grades?"

"Sure," I shoot back, "a football player, or a legacy, or the son of a Duke professor."

Victoria mutters something.

"Didn't hear," says the director.

"I'd just worry about her here. Duke is a place where even the healthiest of girls can develop eating disorders. I'm just afraid."

"That's paternalist bullshit," I hear myself saying to my friend. "We have no right to presume to know how she will respond to the climate at Duke. Our job is to evaluate her candidacy as an applicant, to look at her and decide if we think she can contribute to the community here. She certainly contributed at Calhoun. She's shown that she has the ability to do the work. I don't believe we should penalize her for having been sick. If she'd had a brain tumor instead of anorexia, would we be having this conversation?"

"I'm liking her," says the director. I suspect he's looking again at her testing.

"Listen to her 'Why Duke.' " The director reads, "Because it isn't Yale."

"Okay, okay," says Chuck. "Fine. Let's take her. Rachel's right, we get a lot worse in development rounds."

"Victoria?" the director asks.

"Okay," she says quietly and looks over at me, shaking her head in disapproval of my recklessness.

"Where are my dinosaur stickers?" the director asks. "Let's give Claire a dinosaur."

A dinosaur sticker was placed on the outside of the jacket. The stickers were meant to signal to the folks at the next points in line— housing, premajor advising, student affairs—those applicants whom we admitted but about whom there was concern that they might be at risk in some way, academically, or, as in Claire's case, mentally or emotionally. A number of the kids I wanted to admit were awarded these decorations. Why the stickers were dinosaurs, I have no idea. The director was not without a sense of humor.

He slapped on a brontosaurus, scribbled his initials, and Claire was admitted to Duke.

We move quickly though a bunch of denies and waitlists and a couple of easy admits. Then we get to Dwight Academy.

"Okay," I say, "this school group is a big fat mess."

They can see that, just by looking at the slate.

There are fourteen applicants. The kid who is third from the bottom is a high high. An international student in the middle of the pack had been auto admitted by Audrey, who reads internationals. The top three looked good (and the number two on the slate was coded as medium by the development office). The next two looked like denies, but the sixth kid down, an African American male, looked like a strong admit. There was a low development kid beneath him. Some more denies, and one incomplete.

"Ugh," says Victoria.

"Yeah," I agree.

"So what do you want to do?" the director asks.

"I want to take the top three, deny the next two, take the black guy, and deny the rest. I'm sure the high high guy will be enrolling."

"How about waitlisting those next two from the top?" asks Chuck. "They have higher averages and much, much higher testing than the African American kid."

"No. We're never going to take them off the waiting list. I think we should just cut them loose."

"Let's give them threes as a courtesy to the school," says the director, signing off.

We divided our waitlist decisions into ones, twos, and threes. The WL1s were those that, if we had the room, we wanted to take. They would be the first to be offered places in the class, though after the designation of WL1 there was no ranking of the waiting list, and it was up to each officer to pitch her WL kids when, during the month of May, after the admitted kids had given us their answers, the director asked for them. The twos were the BWRKs, you didn't want to admit them; they were perfectly good so you didn't want to ding them, so you just put them in limbo. They most likely were not going to get in. The WL3s had no chance of admission. They were waitlisted instead of rejected for some reason other than their credentials. Either you thought the school would be pissed off if you denied the "heart and soul of the class," the applicant was the child of an alum (who had given no money and was therefore not entitled to be sent to alumni rounds), or it was simply a great kid and you wanted for purely sentimental reasons, to soften the blow.

I get to a great kid from Cape Cod High School, a kid that I want to take—a fifty-one sum. I want to talk about him, to tell the committee why I think he's so cool. They don't want to hear, at this point. They're happy to take my word and admit him based on my ratings. It's frustrating. We spend very little time talking about the good kids, the clear admits, the kids you want to talk about.

My last big school group from Massachusetts is Morse Academy. I have fifteen applicants and am recommending admitting the top three, waitlisting the next two, and denying the rest.

"Rachel," Chuck says, as I finish talking about the three I want to admit. "These kids are just not that impressive. If they went to a public high school, I don't think you would be arguing to admit them. I think you're buying into these schools' own notions of how great they are, and how wonderful their kids are. Now, maybe I'm missing something here, but these three—I don't see anything special about them. They're BWRKs. And I think you're giving them a boost because you like the school. Which is kind of funny, since you'd be the first to point out how unfair that is. These kids are privileged enough already."

"I think he's right," says Victoria. "I'm kind of surprised that you want to admit these kids. I know what you say about how the sums from your region are deflated because of how hard it is for these kids to be at the top of such competitive classes, and that the teachers tend not to gush as some of the public high school people. But after hearing you describe them, they don't really stand out."

I don't know what stings me more, the fact that I liked these kids—I had met and remembered all of them—and want to get them in or that Chuck and Victoria are exactly right: I had turned into a mere advocate. I had stopped thinking critically. And I had bought into the institutional self-satisfaction that had, during my travels, given me the heebie-jeebies.

"You're right. How about waitlist ones for those three?"

"How about twos," says the director, signing off.

I have finished Massachusetts, and we break for lunch.

California is easier, in a lot of ways, since many of the big feeder schools are excellent public schools that still rank their students and make it easy for us to figure what their grades are like.

The school group for Ross Academy is, as I had suspected, a disaster. There are codes all over the place: alumni, development, athletes. No great kids, plenty of typical ones. We take the ones we have to take and then, to make ourselves feel better, take the top of the school group (who is by no means exceptional).

Stanford High School has sent us twenty-five applicants. Five of them are great, four others perfectly admissible. When looking over the slate from the previous years I saw that they usually sent us good kids, we'd admit them, and then they wouldn't come. This year I argue to move a little farther down the slate, taking kids who, though they aren't quite as good, are more likely to matriculate.

At Mondavi High I have a great Latino applicant, first-gen college. In order to admit him, we take their valedictorian—a typical BWRK with 1390, all As, fine teacher recs, the usual ECs and essays—on his coattails. That will show up on the slate as decision reason Z, or a "coattails decision." When there's a student whom we want to take—for whatever reason, either because they will add diversity to the class or because there is an institutional interest in their application—we feel compelled to admit a "better" student so that school will "understand" the decision.

"Oh boy," I say, when we get to Springfield High. "Here's a kid that I just adore."

"Could you be referring to young Andrew Kaplan, with 1520 boards and a three in achievement?" asks the director.

"Yes. Look, this is a good school. Last year we had ten applicants and we took six of them. None matriculated. This year we only had three apps and I've already auto denied the other two."

"Now," I continue, "what we have left is Andrew Kaplan. Drew took eight APs. Did extremely well in some of them, like physics and biology, and got a C in English. His teachers alternatively call him brilliant and the biggest pain in the ass they have ever encountered. His work is erratic, disorganized, but also often on a much higher level than any of his peers. He makes jokes in class constantly, to the point of disruptiveness. But he's also quick to help slower students understand difficult concepts. He's a short guy who is the star of the basketball team—(his coach wrote a letter)—and he runs hurdles."

"Other than the fact that he's a runner, Rachel, what do you like about him?" Chuck asks, smiling.

"First of all, Chuck, I do not consider hurdlers to be runners. Second, I like *him*. He's very, very smart. He has diagnosed Attention Deficit Disorder, which may account for his grades—can't sit still for very long, is easily bored. But he's funny, very funny, and he's unusual—weird, actually. My sense of him is that he's one of those 'smelly geeks.' "

"What do you mean, 'smelly geeks,' " Chuck asks.

"You know, the guys in college who never figured out that they should be using deodorant. They stank. You would never go out on a date with one, but they were appealing in a quirky sort of way. They were the ones majoring in physics, or math, who would sit outside on nice days and play guitar, or juggle, and they were the ones who came up with elaborate and highly technical pranks and practical jokes. Now they're running the world. You know, like Bill Gates."

"I don't think we have any smelly geeks at Duke," Victoria says.

"Well," I say, "maybe we need some."

"Will you read his essay to the committee?" I ask the director. "Chuck, you are going to love this kid."

The director shuffles through the folder, glaring at me when it became clear that the parts of the application are out of order. Finally he finds the essay and begins reading:

I have wanted to go to Duke for as long as I can remember. My friends and family generally refer to my fascination with Duke as a healthy interest in an outstanding institution. My critics (mainly my overly educated sister (whose greatest strength in life is her capacity to put a negative spin on anything)), call it an obsessive-compulsive neurosis. The two areas of my life that most reflect this deep and abiding interest in Duke are the names of my pets and my wardrobe.

When I was 5 years old I first became interested in Duke by sitting with my older brother (who was forced to baby-sit me against his wishes) while he watched Duke basketball games. I had no idea what was going on but I gradually figured out that it was really good when someone with a blue shirt on threw the ball into the basket. I was given a goldfish for my 6th birthday. I named it "Duke." Soon it died and I got another goldfish. I named it "Duke" also. At one point I had 5 goldfish (my parents had little imagination and my sister believes that they tried to compensate for the fact that they were never around by buying us goldfish). At first I named them "Duke1," "Duke2," "Duke3," "Duke4," "Duke5." I had tremendous difficulty figuring out which was which and after a while I gave up and just called them all "Duke."

Around this time I started asking for Duke paraphernalia and clothing with the "Duke" logo. Soon I refused to wear anything if it didn't say "Duke" on it. I started to become interested in school and became aware of the excellent academics at Duke. While other boys my age stayed awake at night fantasizing about girls, I thought about going to Duke.

A couple of years later my parents got me a puppy (you don't want to know what my sister said about that). The name "Duke" was in use by several goldfish at the time so I had to come up with something else. I decided on "Mike Krzyzewski." This was a big mistake. My sister tormented me mercilessly for repeatedly mispronouncing the name of my own dog. She would say, "it's shi-shev-sky, not cri-zew-ski." For years I insisted that "it couldn't possibly be shi-shev-sky if it started with a K". I was greatly relieved to learn that many people referred to him as "Coach K." Soon Coach K died (he was sadly hit by a car). Immediately afterwards my parents got me a new puppy (my sister said they did this so they wouldn't have to deal with my grief over Coach K). Once again I was faced with a serious problem. Thirty goldfish had dibs on "Duke" (with all my experience, I had become an expert goldfish breeder (one of my fish was awarded 3rd prize in a national goldfish competition)) and I was too heart-broken still to call another dog Coach K. Before I had come up with a name for the puppy and before she was house-trained, I received a call from my sister at school telling me that I'd better get my bottom home right away because the puppy had just pooped on my mother's brand new $20,000 Persian rug. I cut class and sprinted home in a state of terror. The rug was all white with a small dark design in the center. I could hardly breathe by the time I got home. I walked in the front door and immediately began trying to clean the rug. It was a miracle! The puppy had pooped only on the dark part of the rug! It cleaned up without a trace! I decided to name the puppy Christian Laettner because the puppy had made a miracle Shot. Unfortunately, this time my sister teased me mercilessly because I had given a female dog a male name. Oh well. There's just no satisfying some people.

You can clearly see that I have been the most avid of Duke fans for a long time. I hope to go to College at Duke to be a part of all of its excitement and greatness. I also have a practical reason why I need to go to Duke. I am now at the point where every article of clothing in my wardrobe (including my underwear) has "Duke" imprinted or sewn on it. If I am not accepted to Duke I will have to attend the University of North Carolina. At UNC I will be ostracized if I wear clothes that say "Duke" on them and will, therefore, be unable to wear ANY of my clothes. I would have to buy a whole new wardrobe and there is no way that I will be able to afford that for the next two years (until my sister graduates from Yale) since things are so financially tight in my family. So please. Have compassion on me. Fulfill my greatest fantasy and allow me to attend college at Duke. Do not force me to go clothes-less to Chapel Hill.

"He's insane," says Chuck. "I love it."

"He is very funny," confesses Victoria.

"He's got good board scores," I add weakly.

The director looks up.

"Well, committee, what do you think?"

"Are you actually suggesting that we admit him?" Victoria asks me.

"Well, yes. I love him. I think he'd add a quirky perspective to the student body here. I suspect he'd be more at home at MIT or Caltech, who will no doubt take him. But I have to say, I just love him."

Chuck is still giggling. Finally he sobers up. "Rachel, are you actually going to ask us to admit a kid ranked thirty-four in his class, with Bs and Cs after you've just had us deny a string of appli-

cants who were in the top 5 percent—and in the top 2 percent—
of their classes with the same board scores; kids you didn't want
to admit because they were boring BWRKs, and now you think we
should take this guy because Duke needs more smelly geeks?
Come on, now."

For a twenty-three-year-old kid, Chuck was amazingly adept at
putting me in my place.

"Do you have midterm grades on this guy?" the director
asks me.

We were supposed to track down the midterm grades of all
applicants. In practice, we did it where we thought they'd help;
either help to get a kid admitted because they'd gone up, or help
in the argument to keep someone out. I had, of course, looked for
Drew's midterm grades. They were not in his file, so I called the
school to get them.

"Well," I hesitate. "Yes, I do."

"Were you going to share them with the committee?"
Chuck asks.

"An A in AP physics," and then I muttered "three Bs and a C in
English. But at least it was a C plus."

They look at me.

"How about a teeny tiny little waitlist, then," I ask, meekly,
knowing I was going to lose this one.

"Committee, do you want to waitlist this smelly geek?" the
director asks.

"Oh, why not," Victoria says finally.

"Chuck?"

"Just don't let her have a WL1 on him. I'll agree if he's no higher than a WL2. I keep thinking about that poor Val we just denied who was a 55433 with a 1430. And the kid Rachel didn't like before him who was third in the class and president of the Conservative Students Union. And the perfectly fine young woman from Monte Santos who had all As and wrote her essay about her Hungarian father and was a dancer that we denied. And the kid from the all-boys Catholic school that Rachel thought was a grade grubber, you remember, the Eagle Scout with 1540 boards who went to Boys State? And the also the—"

I cut him off.

"Okay, okay, okay. A WL2 for my smelly geek Drew Kaplan. Fine. Can we move on now?" I pretend to glare at Chuck, but he is smiling so broadly that I laugh.

At Coastal High I am stymied.

"Okay, I want to ask for the committee's help on this one. Nathan Sims is a 55434 with a five in testing—he's got a 1550 and a bunch of high seven hundreds on his SAT IIs. I don't much like him. I think he's boring. I'm inclined to want to waitlist him. But the guidance counselor told me that parents are reluctant to have their kids apply because the word is that we never take applicants from this school. Nathan is one of their best; he's second in the class. If we were going to take any of them, he would be the one."

"What are his ECs?" asks Chuck.

"Well, he's the president of JSA, captain of debate. He doesn't play any sports, but he does do the announcing at football and basketball games. He started an investment club. And he plays the violin."

"Did he send in a supplemental music tape?"

"Yeah, he did. It came back from the music department with a four. They said they could use a violinist like him in the symphony. He's not great, but he is accomplished."

"What were his essays on?" Victoria asks.

"The two shorts ones were completely typical. The long essay wasn't bad, but it was about how much he admired Milton Friedman."

"I see," says the director.

"You see what?" I ask innocently.

"What do his teachers say?" asks Chuck.

"They like him. They say he's the best this year. Worked very hard, had lots of questions, clearly thinking at a higher level than his peers. 'Made my job more challenging, but also more enjoyable.' Never accepts an easy answer. Motivated, mature. Attained impressive levels of understanding."

"I'm liking this guy," says Chuck. "I don't think we should take him because of the counselor's comments to Rachel about what the parents think, but I do think we should take him on his own merits. Sure, he's a BWRK, but he's a strong BWRK. I think he deserves to be admitted. By they way, who is Milton Friedman?"

"Who let you into Duke?" I ask Chuck.

"Do you have room for him in your numbers?" Victoria wonders.

"Yeah, I think so, since I had counted on being able to get Drew Kaplan past you guys."

"Why don't we give him an Ao and see where we are at the end. If we have room, we'll take him."

The director signs off and hands the folder to Chuck.

In the area around Silicon Valley, I had a lot of Asian applicants, not surprisingly. Lots of high testing and lots of teacher recommendations that complained about the student's lack of class participation. While there were plenty of Asian Americans who did lots of cool extracurricular activities, many of the first-generation Americans didn't. After school they'd work in family-owned stores or do church-related activities. Their reader ratings were typically flat on the end. A five in curriculum choice, a five in achievement, usually a four in Recs (good written work but too quiet in class), and then threes for essays and extracurriculars. With a five on the end for testing. 554335. Typical Asian kid. I tried hard to make sure that they were getting a fair read. But they were much of a muchness. This was a problem we didn't address.

During the course of regular rounds, a day was set aside for engineering rounds. The process was a bit different, much more numbers driven. We would receive printed labels with the applicant's name, their engineering sum, and their decision. If they were an eighty-eight sum or above, their decision would be admit. If they were below a sixty-seven sum, they would be a deny. If we agreed with these decisions, we simply slapped the label on the jacket and sent it down for processing.

For those who we thought the numbers should not dictate the decision, we were allowed to present their applications to the committee of engineers. We were given explicit instructions about how to speak to these people; told by the director to "watch me" for silent signals about what to say and when to shut up. They sat in the director's office, these professors, usually four white men with white hair. Each admissions officer would enter in turn. We pitched to them; they talked to each other.

Chuck had a kid whose alumni interview report actually made a difference in the way he read the application, and so he decided to bring him before the engineers. John Mack was from a school in Pittsburgh that hadn't sent us many applications, so Chuck wasn't familiar with it. It turned out, from reading the interview report that even though the kid was technically from Pittsburgh, he lived in a very rural area.

John had maxed out the math and science courses available to him, including AP calc, physics, and chem. He got a C in English junior year; Bs in English in 10 and 12. Had 780 math, 600 verbal, thus giving him a three in engineering testing; four plus in recs from math and science teachers. His extracurriculars had stopped abruptly junior year. The alumni interviewer sussed out that this was because his father had decided to build an addition onto their house. He expected John to come home right after school every day and help him with it. It hadn't occurred to John to mention this on his application, and he didn't see it as a punishment. He was more interested in the engineering aspects of building than he was in playing in the band. Chuck explained to the committee that his SATs were low because the school hadn't properly prepared him, and that he was the first person in his family to apply to college. He also pointed out the Cs in English. A ruddy-faced engineering professor said, "Hell, I made a C in high school English. That doesn't bother me." Even though he had a seventy-four sum, the committee was persuaded to take him.

Victoria was arguing for a young man with a lowish sum, but he had gone to a stinky high school and had worked very hard. They kept looking at his SATs and SAT IIs and shaking their heads. Finally she pleaded, he's a poet.

"Ah," said an old Russian engineer. "A poet. We need more poets in engineering. Why don't we take this young man?"

And he was in.

After rounds were over, there was a lot of cleanup to be done. Applications that were not complete had either to be completed— by calling the applicant and telling them (again—they'd already been sent a "lacking" card telling them what was missing) that they were incomplete or by deciding to cancel their application. A few late reads trickled in from the first readers.

Then there was the preparation for alum and development rounds. This meant going through the list of coded applicants in your region and pulling out a whole bunch of information, most of which would never be looked at. You had to fill out a form that had information about the high school's impression of the applicant; whether the school was aware of any "special circumstances" that might affect a decision; how a decision to admit would be viewed by the school. You also had to provide copies of the past three years of history on the school—the sums of the lowest regular admit, and the lowest "special" kids, mostly development or alumni admits. The director never wanted to admit these kids and had to fight to be able to keep them out. He usually lost. He wanted to make sure that the admissions officer gave him as much ammunition as possible to use against them. He'd make sure we looked for midterm grades and new testing. He was not much interested in our personal opinions of the applicant and didn't give an opportunity to express them. That rarely stopped us.

Alum and development rounds consisted of the director, the head of the university's development office, and the Alumni liaison to admissions. Alumni were coded as either A or B. An A meant that they had been active and involved with the school since graduation; often this meant that they had a history of consistent giving, but also rewarded were the good soldiers who showed up for reunions and were involved in their local alumni clubs. The alum B category got less of a boost—it simply meant that these people kept their records and whereabouts up-to-date with the alumni office. And then there were the alum Xs. The alumni office had lost track of them, so even if a kid had written on her application that her parent had gone to Duke, it didn't help. Development codes were high, for those who had not only the potential to give loads of money, but who had a history of giving it to Duke; medium, those who also had loads of money, had never given it to Duke, but had given to similar kinds of places; and low, which could mean that the family was rich but not philanthropic, or that someone somewhere (usually fairly high up, could be a trustee, could be the basketball coach) had some kind of personal interest in the application. These kids were always discussed, but the director often triumphed in keeping them out.

Alum and development rounds were usually an all-day affair. We were allowed to sit in and to speak only if spoken to. It was hard to remain silent, and sometimes I failed. But the process gave a good overview of long-term institutional goals and the directions of the university, a big picture focus that we the foot soldiers in admissions were rarely privy to. Here we would learn about plans for a new Center for Jewish Life, a Genomics Institute, an addition to the gym. These planning goals were being made possible by large gifts, and although there was never a quid pro quo for donors with children applying, the development office wanted to be sure that everything possible was done for them. So they arranged special tours and VIP interviews for these applicants (didn't help them, but it made them feel special), and then they came into rounds to plead their cases.

The kids who went to these special rounds had already been denied, either as auto denies or in committee. They were, without a doubt, the weakest portion of our applicant pool. Sitting in on the rounds could be highly amusing—the director of development was a smart, very funny man. It could also be tense. The director had to reserve a number of places in the class for these kids, places that could easily have been filled by regular kids whom we then had to deny in rounds. Our target numbers for our regions were deflated; even though I was only able to admit forty kids from Massachusetts, once you took into account the athletes and the alum and development admits, the final number would be much greater.

Most admissions officers hated to see these kids get in. I know I did. Occasionally you'd find a kid you liked whom you knew wasn't going to make it on her own. Those you hoped might be coded. That happened rarely. More often they were arrogant, entitled, or just plain not smart enough for you to want to have them admitted and take a place from a more deserving kid. The biggest problem with admitting so many of these truly mediocre kids—

they made the BWRKs look like fascinating geniuses—was that when they were admitted they usually matriculated. Though the top tier of our applicant pool generally turned us down for other schools, the alum and development kids were lucky to get in and came. The Duke student body was disproportionately heavy with them.

The weakest of the weak applicants—those who didn't make it through alum and development rounds but had some kind of major push behind them—went to provost's rounds, the court of last resort.

As the process reached completion, the targets hit from each region, the director would put out calls for "build in." There was a complicated regression analysis model that told him how many admits he needed to fill the class. So of the fourteen thousand or so applicants, we would admit around thirty-eight hundred, to yield a class of sixteen hundred. He left room in the class after rounds, after all the athletes, development admits, and other hooked applicants had been counted, for tweaking. He'd send out E-mails: "Bring me more high-testing Asians." "I need more 'impact' kids, more exciting kids to talk about in my convocation speech." "We must have more admits from California, Texas, and Florida." "We need to pull back twenty North Carolinians—we admitted too many in rounds—my mistake."

We were also able to bring to him kids we were losing sleep over. Admissions officers often worried about decisions after they were made. The director encouraged this hyperresponsibility by saying that you could always come to him if you wanted to rediscuss an applicant. He realized that committee decisions were sometimes affected by intangibles like the dynamics of the personalities involved, the time of day the decision was being made, and the role blood-sugar levels played. So he was open to hearing appeals. And we did appeal. You had to present your argument to him: You could do it orally, but most of us realized that it was better and more persuasive to write a memo and attach it to the file. That way he could read over everything and spend more time making the decision.

At this point, he gave us our opportunity to pitch to him our "wild card." We got to choose among our applicants a kid that we really wanted to admit who had not made it through selection committee. It should be, he warned, a kid who is admissible, probably from among the WLIs.

Everyone had a wild card. The senior associate surprised us all with hers: an African American guy with lots of Cs on his transcript and less than stellar testing. But he had sung TV commercial jingles, had written and published a novel, and had spent a summer with the Dance Theater of Harlem. He also worked twenty hours a week to help support his family. He was admitted.

I had a wild card. It was Shawn White, the kid I'd met at my Berkeley Duke night. She'd applied early decision, and I'd had to fight like hell to have her deferred rather than denied outright. As it turned out, her circumstances were indeed complex. In her tenth grade year her best friend committed suicide. Her mother remarried. Shawn had failed out of high school in North Carolina. She became depressed and stopped going to class. As a last ditch she went to live with her family friends in Oakland and enrolled in a city school.

There was a wonderful letter from her History teacher (also her basketball coach). She described first noticing Shawn: "She was white. One of about three white kids in a school of fifteen hundred." Then she started hearing about her from other teachers. Shawn had resurrected the school newspaper, becoming editor in chief, started a school coffeehouse, and sang in the Gospel choir. She also went out for basketball. Her teacher talked about the reaction of the team: "What's that skinny white girl doing, coach, she got no game?" Shawn quickly won over her teammates with her willingness to work hard and to not take herself too seriously.

Her application was wonderful. For her "why Duke," she had mocked up a copy of the school paper. Usually this is a bad move. They are almost always cheesy. Not Shawn's. The headline was something like WHITE APPLIES TO DUKE. Also on the front page was a story, SHAWN WHITE'S BATTLE WITH DEPRESSION, that jumped to an inside page. The head was DEPRESSION CONTINUED. It was ironic and it was funny and it was sweet.

She had made all As in her new school. Her testing was solid for a North Carolinian, though weak in the rest of the applicant pool.

To the surprise of everyone, the director admitted her. But not before placing three dinosaur stickers on the application jacket.

9

April Is the Cruelest Month: *Decisions*

"Every girl I know at Duke keeps a quote book," my friend
Lauren, a junior from south of Boston, told me recently.
Many girls, she says, started in high school. Their books
range in format from hastily penned scribbles in spiral
notebooks to elaborate entries in designerly cloth covers;
all contain collections of quotations (which the kids call
"quotes," not recognizing a verb-noun difference). Lauren
showed me hers. It contains quotations she's come across
in books, mostly with attributions (lots from Thoreau),
but some without; things she's heard professors say in
class; comments by friends; and copies of E-mail mes-
sages needing to be saved in some sort of permanent
fashion.

   While it surprised me to learn about this contemporary
practice, I guess it's not really an innovation. For centuries
young people had "copy books," in which a heading at the
top of the page would be followed by blank space for the
obsessive transcription of a quotation. The double purpose

was to practice handwriting and to instill moral values, or perhaps just fear: "The wages of sin is death," for example.

When it came time to put away childish things, the copy book was replaced by its close cousin, the "commonplace book." The process of maturation required the production of more personal collections of writings, meant to provide inspiration, direction, and moral fortitude. Reading the commonplace books of historical figures like George Washington, Thomas Jefferson, or any number of antebellum Southern ladies gives us an interior view of each person's self-image and the words that motivate him or her.

The urge to be self-reflective seems to be expressed most easily by using the words of others. Growing up is about shaking off the accents of the familial home and learning new patterns of speech. It's about developing your own voice, but it's hard enough to figure out what you want to say; finding a new and insightful way to say it is a big burden. So it appeals, this quoting, finding tidbits of truth, expressed by others more confident with language. And, at a time when life is often overwhelming, it's reassuring to find and hold on to those sayings that provide guidance, inspiration, or maybe even just a giggle.

Even those students who do not keep track of quotations in private journals are on the lookout for good sayings. Dorm-room doors boast white boards with "quote of the day" sections; common rooms have forums for people to write the favorite things they've heard or read; student papers often begin with a quotation. Such public quoting is different from the interiority of private scribbling. It says something about you, not to you. It makes a statement, and (as we all remember from our college years) making a statement is an important part of this phase of development. See how intellectual I am? See how cynical and worldly the inhabitants of this Nietzsche-quoting dorm are? I'm unique! I've got a bizzaro sense of humor! These public quotes are bumper stickers for people who don't spend a lot of time in cars.

Perhaps, in a couple of centuries, historians will be looking through Lauren's quote book and getting a bead on life at the beginning of a new millennium. They may have to do some digging to contextualize Bart Simpson and Leo Buscaglia, Ani DiFranco and SARK. My guess is that it won't be immediately clear, a couple of hundred years from now, what chicken soup has to do with the soul. But the use of quotations will say something to posterity about this generation of college students.

I have made a number of friends among the Duke students. I seek them out. I want to know if the Duke I described while recruiting actually exists or if it is my imagined vision of what Duke could be. It's a little of both. The kids welcome the contact. They're friendly, outgoing, and generally socially graceful. This time of year, when the flowers are in bloom and the Frisbees are flying, lots of people hang out on the quad. I have no hesitation about going up to random students and questioning them on their Duke experience.

I'd like to be out there now, but instead Victoria and I are sitting on the floor of my office doing PDP, or post-decision processing. We've got the denies, D–G. They're easy, as PDP goes: just a one-page letter to be stuffed into a skinny envelope. We have to check the name and address against the master list, file the yellow copy inside the jacket, and stuff the letter. After three months of intense reading, it's kind of fun to do manual, mindless labor.

I read off the names and Victoria checks.

"Darren Darst," I say, spelling the last name. She checks, we stuff.

"Okay."

"Jasmine Daschel. D-A-S-C-H-E-L"

"Okay."

"Brian Deets. D-E-E-T-S"

"Okay."

"Sara Delancy."

"Sara without a final *h*?"

"Yep."

"Okay."

"Thomas Doniphon. D-O-N-I-P-H-O-N."

"You're kidding—we denied a kid named Tom Doniphon?"

"Yeah, why?"

"He's the man who shot Liberty Valance."

"Well, that didn't get him into Duke. Charles Duncan."

"Oh, he's one of mine," I say.

"Yeah?" She looks up.

"Sucked!" I say. She bursts into giggles.

We go on like this. Occasionally discussing our own applicants when we come across them. Mostly I say "sucked!" each time we find one of mine (whom I remember). Sometimes we have a little elegy for the sweet kids we liked, but who we knew were never going to get into Duke. We don't always remember the kids from our regions who were auto denied and therefore never discussed in committee.

Before the letters hit, we have a staff meeting to discuss the inevitable ensuing discussions.

"Never say that an applicant was rejected," admonishes the director. "Never even say that they were denied. Say instead, we're terribly sorry but we weren't able to admit you. They'll take it personally enough as it is, we don't want them to feel worse.

"When an applicant calls, do not speak with him or her until you have the file in front of you. Don't try to wing it, and don't speak just from your yellow sheet. You must have the file. If they want to know what was wrong with their application, be as helpful as you can. Nine times out of ten if you just give them the strength-of-the-pool line, that will suffice. If someone, usually it will be a parent, becomes abusive, tell them that you are unable to continue the conversation at this time but that you will be happy to have them call back when they are more calm.

"Don't let people come away from a conversation thinking that we have devalued the academic (or extracurricular) accomplishments of their children. Instead, use the data as a way of gently educating people that because their child applied to a school with a very talented applicant pool, there are many outstanding and capable students we just weren't able to admit, even though we wish we could.

"Keep in mind, too, we are not out to win any arguments about whether our decision was a good one or not. It was, of course, not a good one from the caller's point of view, and there is little we can say to convince them otherwise. And realistically speaking, virtually all of our applicants could do just fine here, so the parents are not far off base. They just don't have the advantage of knowing the context—the strength of our pool. So please, be sympathetic, understanding, and friendly.

"For those who walk in to the office to get their decisions, take them to a private place—it doesn't have to be your office—and get a copy of the letter from the file and give it to them. This is, of course, only for the denies and waitlists. If the applicant has been admitted, you can simply tell them."

Every year the skinny denies and waitlist envelopes are mailed out a day or two before the big thick priority-mail admit packs. The thinking is that they should both hit around the same time. This year, as it turns out, the admit packs were delayed in the post office. So while the vast majority of students got their skinny letters, many of their friends were still waiting to hear.

What fun. A student would call. The women in the phone room would ask where they go to high school and then put them through to the regional officer. I would almost always recognize the name, but before I'd give the decision I would go into the database. Social Security number? I'd ask, and they always had it handy. It took the computer a few seconds to think, and there'd be tense silence on the phone. I'm just waiting for the computer to pull up the information, I'd tell them, and in response I'd get a soft murmur. Finally, there it would be: ADT.

"Jessica," I'd say, "I'm delighted to tell you that you have been offered a place in the class." Then I'd hold the phone away from my ear, for invariably there would be screams of delight. "Thank you, thank you, thank you so much," she'd say.

A few days later, after everyone had his or her decision, I'd get more calls. Some truly moving thanks from parents—especially of weaker applicants. "I know how much you did for Nick," a mom said, "and I want you to know that I appreciate it."

In general, though, these days when the phone rings it is not good. A small fraction of the calls are actually from students. Mostly it is parents who call. "How could you reject him?" an irate dad would ask. "He's in the top ten percent of his class. He had 1380 SATs. He played varsity baseball and was captain of debate. This is an outrage." They want to appeal. They always wanted to appeal, especially the lawyer parents. There was a formal process, a request for reconsideration. They had to prove that there was something procedurally wrong with the review of the application— a teacher rec, say, was missing from the file. Otherwise, our decisions stood.

Sometimes they wanted to talk not only about their child's admissions fate, but to demand to know why Johnny, their son's friend, got in instead. His grades aren't as good, they'd say. His SATs were lower, they'd plead. The policy is never to talk about other applicants. What could you say—well, but Johnny's parents have given 1.5 million dollars to the school over the past few years. Some of the parents just wanted you to tell them what they could say to their kids to console them. That was easy—it was simply about the strength of the pool and had nothing to do with any flaws in their child's application. But those angry calls, giving you the rundown on the very credentials you had used to deny an applicant, those were hard to take. "You said your middle 50 percent was 1350 to 1520. My child had a 1380. Why didn't she get in?" What could you say, that the kids below 1480 were generally alum and development admits, underrepresented minorities, athletes? No. You just said that you were very, very sorry and that you knew little Iodine would do well wherever she ended up.

The phone rings. I pick it up.

"Rachel, thankyousomuch."

"Um, you're welcome," I say. "And who is this?"

"It's Katie, Katie Ross. We met at the Duke night in Boston."

"Oh, of course." Though I didn't remember meeting her, I did recall her application. She was a dancer, second in her public school class of four hundred something and she'd written a raw and emotional essay on the death of a close friend. "Hey, Katie, how's it going?"

"Great! I just got my fat envelope. I am so happy."

"So does that mean you'll be coming to Duke?"

"My dad has already written out the check."

"Well, look, I'm coming up to Boston next week for the party for accepted students. You'll be invited. I hope you come to it."

"I will! I will! And thank you," she bubbles.

"No," I say, honestly, "thank you. Your application made my day."

Each spring the alumni office organizes parties for admitted students, held around the country at the homes of dutiful Duke alumni. They send faculty and administrators to these parties, ostensibly to give a talk that will generate excitement and convince the kids to matriculate. Unfortunately these talks were not always as enthusiastic as the alumni hoped. In fact, a couple of the alumni committees requested that an administrator or faculty member *not* be sent to their party. Admissions officers were asked if they wanted to attend. I most certainly did. Not only because I wanted to meet "my kids," especially the applicants I'd fallen in love with on paper, but also, because the party was set to take place the day before the Boston Marathon. What could be better, I thought, to be sent up there for a work function and then, since I was in the neighborhood, to run the marathon.

Before I leave I do my homework. I make a list of all the kids we'd admitted who are likely to show up at the party. On this list I note salient facts about them: Brian Peele—cross-country runner, wrote about Margeret, his anorexic cousin; Winston Chang, engineer, got five on Vergil AP test—hockey player who wrote about space-time physics—not a good driver (he'd written his long essay on getting in a car accident); Daria Williams—born-again Christian feminist rower with 1540 boards—feminist reading of *Memoirs of a Geisha*—plays ice hockey; Francie Martini—classicist, coxswain—worked in ice-cream shop—independent study on women in the ancient world; Ahmet Sa'ad—"There is no fly fishing club at Duke; that will change"—sax-playing debater—incredible writer; Jason Roth—artsy runner—launched full-scale production of *Volpone* at his high school, wrote about going to both church and temple; Rachel McGinley—gymnastics, head of gay-straight alliance— "Every day I am grateful for Title IX"; Martin Breslick—black belt in karate, has met with Kofi Anan, Madeline Albright, and me.

Did I want to meet these kids? You bet I did.

So I made my plans to go to Boston and began my taper for the marathon.

Meanwhile, back in the office, admitted students began to drop by. At first they'd be mostly local, but as the days since the letters hit passed, we'd get more and more. It was fun to patrol the lobby looking for admitted students. At the same time, the big crowds of juniors began to appear, just starting their college search. When doing the group, I always asked if there were any newly admitted students.

We are gearing up for Blue Devil Days, the program for admitted students. After months of being supplicants, applicants are now in the position of power and have the ability to choose. We use these days to try to convince them to come to Duke. It's a series of dog and pony shows. We trot out the most engaging faculty members and the most well spoken undergraduates to talk to these kids and their families. Each morning of the eight days of the program, there would be a kickoff speaker. It's supposed to be someone impressive, whose very presence would signal to families how important this recruiting business was. Sometimes they were great.

The best thing about Blue Devil Days is the weather. It is sunny and warm in Durham during the month of April, and the architectural beauty of the campus is enhanced by thousands of blossoming trees and flowers. The admissions staff sets up tables in the student center, usually a couple of members of the "operations" staff, secretaries anxious to escape the drudgery of the office, are assigned to help check in students when they arrive and give them packages of information. A number of us spend every day on campus, hanging out, seeing current students, and scoping for our own applicants.

When they check in, students are asked for their address; this makes it easy for the admissions officers.

"Hey, Rach," Audrey calls out, "here's one of yours."

"Hi, who are you?"

"Um, Adam Rosen" the handsome, tall young man said.

"Oh my god," I screech. (I have been known to screech.) "The guy who wrote about the physics of Frisbees? I'm so glad to meet you."

His parents look on, speechless.

"I read your application. I read all the applications from Massachusetts. You go to West High, right?"

"Yes," he says hesitantly, looking at me as if I were insane.

"And you wrote your book essay about John McPhee and you play the trumpet."

"How do you know all this?"

"I just told you, I read your application."

He still looks a little puzzled.

"What are you planning to do today?" I say, looking over his shoulder at the schedule he'd been given.

"Well, I was planning to sit in on a class. Any recommendations?"

"Come sit down with me."

I was surprised to see him at Blue Devil Days. This kid was a great kid, an auto admit. I figured that he would turn us down for an Ivy League school; only about a quarter of our top applicants end up matriculating at Duke.

Most of the families are happy and friendly; the months of waiting and agonizing and worrying had paid off, and here they were. Many of them come up to me, telling me that they'd met me when I came to their high school in the fall, or they had come to one of my Duke nights. I also had kids say that they'd been in an information session that I'd led on campus. It was a happy time for everyone.

I fly up to Boston, a little reluctant to leave the festivities of recruiting our admitted applicants.

The party for accepted students was held in a lovely home in Newton, and attendance was great—about twenty-five kids and their families came. The Boston alum who'd been at my Duke night was there, and he said a few words of welcome. Then he turned the program over to me, and I was on.

"In this room we have Eagle Scouts, dancers, gold medalists in the Science Olympiad, a Junior Olympic fencer, a born-again Christian feminist rower, two people who have run the Boston Marathon, the author of a vegetarian cookbook for kids, a National Champion Show Jumper, a card-carrying member of the ACLU, a handful of black belts in karate and in tae kwon do, a quilter, the anchor of his own TV sports show, a drum major, a female wrestler, a huge number of editors in chiefs, captains of sports teams, presidents of clubs, and every single one of you is a member of National Honor Society.

"You all took hard classes and did extremely well. Your teachers promised that you could walk on water. And your essays moved me, sometimes to tears, made me laugh, and let me understand who you are. Dan, over there, I said, pointing to a short guy in the back, began his essay: "Six feet. That's what I wanted to be." He wrote about how and why he wanted to be six feet tall. His essay was about not growing, and about the ways in which he has grown. I loved it. Sally wrote about the U.S. Navy bombings of Vieques. How many of us even know where Vieques is? Josh wrote about his friendship with a forty-year-old woman. Bob wrote about his summer job, collecting trash at Fenway Park. Mandy wrote about what it was like to be an openly gay high school student. Ryan wrote about sitting on second base, thinking.

"How did I know which of all the applicants I wanted to argue most forcefully to be admitted to Duke? It was those I wanted to hang out with, the kids I thought my friends on the faculty would most enjoy teaching, the ones I thought would benefit from and contribute to our diverse community. In short, I wanted you to be admitted, and now I want you to come. You will be in good company. Look around. You may be looking at the best friend you will ever have.

"And don't forget this: if you do come to Duke, I want you to stop by my office and fill me in on how you are doing.

"Oh yeah, and one more thing," I said.

"I'm running the Boston Marathon tomorrow. I know that you all have the day off from school. I hope that you will be out on the course and that if you see me, you will cheer!"

That got an immediate and spontaneous cheer, and soon I was swarmed with both students and parents wanting to know my number, to hear where I qualified for the race and what pace I was hoping to run. Boston has the most astute marathon spectators of any place in the world. Most of the people at the party told me that they watch the race every year. They all said they would look out for me.

The mingling began. Groups started to form. I found Dom, my funeral home Doogie Howser.

Hey, Dom," I said to him, "you're going to need to get a work-study job, right?"

"Yeah," he said. "I'll probably end up mopping floors in the hospital."

"Well look," I said. "My ex-boyfriend Andrew is a doctor on the faculty of Duke. Each year he hires work-study students to help him with his research. If you're interested, I can suggest that he hire you."

"Interested? Are you kidding? That would be great!"

"Yeah, I think you'd like him a lot. And chances are, by the end of your first year he will have you listed as a coauthor on a medical journal article."

They'd hit it off, I thought. And Andrew is a great mentor.

Redheaded Lauren came bounding up to me. I knew from her application that she was an outstanding student, super organized, mature, and responsible. Meeting her in person showed her to be vivacious and warm and likable. I took her aside.

"Lauren, are you going to be looking for a work-study job next year?" I knew that since she had applied for financial aid, she would be.

"Yes, though I guess I haven't really thought about it at all."

"Well, I wanted to plant a seed in your head. I'm going to hire a student to work with me in admissions, to try to recruit the top tier of our applicant pool. I'd love to have someone like you help me with that project."

"Oh, wow, that would be great!"

Four guys, all good kids, all on the short side, gelled into a cluster. By the time it was time to leave, they had made plans to go to a Red Sox game.

I ran well the next day, and I heard my name several times on the marathon course. I saw Muffy, the counselor from Ezra Stiles and another from a Catholic girls school I'd visited. A few miles later there were a bunch of the Stiles guys holding a big sign that said, "ES loves Duke! Rachel Toor! Number 6383!" One of the moms handed me a bottle of water. I was wearing a Duke singlet that had been loaned to me by the track coach just for the occasion. When I ran past Wellesley College, the Wellesley women who traditionally cheer extra loud for female marathoners, screamed "Go, Duke!" It took me a few moments to realize that meant "Go, Rachel!"

Back at home, Blue Devil Days over, we check the return cards that come daily in the mail. The cards tell us which schools the applicant applied to, where they were admitted, and where they will be matriculating. I am surprised at how personally I take it when a kid turns us down for another school. But then I remember the conversations I'd had about financial aid. Many of these people, especially middle-class families, got much better need-based financial aid offers from other schools. For some reason, Duke's "need-based" aid policy seems to be less generous than others. And there are schools who do "preferential packaging," giving more money to the kids they want to attend.

I stand in the office of the data entry clerks, two African American women who seem to have infinite patience and shuffle through the cards.

"Oh no," I let out.

"What? What?" They ask.

"Just a kid who's turned us down," I say, looking at the card that bears Claire Hess's name and the information that she will be matriculating at Yale. Drat.

I find the card for John Osborne, my nationally ranked archer. He'll be going to Princeton. And my California feminist Amelia will be going to Swarthmore. Drat. Drat. Drat.

I find a card for Justin Brandon, the Ross football player I'd met at my Berkeley Duke night. I had been right about him; his academic credentials were terribly weak, nothing higher than a three in his reader ratings and a couple of twos. His application had gone to development rounds. He would, it seemed, be coming to Duke.

I learn that there had been a snafu with some of the denies. John Davis had gotten Patricia David's letter. The stuffing had not been accurate. It's hard enough to be rejected, but to get someone else's rejection letter and to have to call and find out about both your own rejection and the incompetence of the admissions staff (it may be remembered that I was the one stuffing those D denies), that's a low blow. I feel terrible. I dread that the phone will ring and I will have to find out about more careless but heart-wrenching mistakes we—I—had made.

The phone does keep on ringing. Most of the calls are from students (and parents of students) placed on the waiting list. There are thousands of them, and while we can tell, maybe, how much of a chance they have by looking up to see the level of their waitlist (WL1, WL2 or WL3), they have no way of knowing.

And so they call and write, long letters telling us of any small achievements they had accomplished since their application had been sent in: "I was elected homecoming queen"; "I got a B+ in physics"; "I'm finishing my term on the honor roll again." Mostly what they express is just their interest in attending Duke if admitted. This is not such a bad idea, since we will want to offer places to those who will accept them. So we each keep files on our desks of eager waitlist hopefuls. We won't know until early May how many more applicants we'll be able to admit; it depends on how many accepted students decided to matriculate. The number will be something between zero and a couple hundred. It's only the WL1s who have any sort of chance. And there are thousands of them.

Just when you think reading is finished, more folders appear on your desk.

"Rachel," the director's secretary says, "I need you to read this football player for me."

"It's May," I respond. "Didn't anyone tell him that applications were due in January?"

"Oh, he's already been admitted. But he just sent in the completed application, and now it has to be read."

"Does it occur to anyone that this system is a little backward?"

But for the revenue sports, football and basketball, that's how it works. Get admitted, make a commitment, then apply.

So we read our football players, finish up the waiting list, and figure out who will be on our campus next year and who is going on to Harvard, or to be a Jefferson Scholar at University of Virginia, or is taking a year off to go trekking in Nepal. Some applicants apply to have their matriculation deferred for a year. We almost always grant those requests.

Then we have to start giving the humongous groups again— talking to eager juniors and their parents as the flowers continue to bloom and the Duke students clear out of campus for summer jobs and European vacations.

For us rookies, now we are giving the group knowing a lot more about the admissions process. What we know, too, is that most of the kids to whom we are speaking have a better chance of being hit by lightning than they do of getting into Duke. You can't help but think of all the committee-denied valedictorians and high 1500s kids when parents start asking about the strength of their children's candidacy. So you put on a happy face and talk about how the SAT is just one of the things we look at, how great the academics are, and how much fun it is to see basketball games in Cameron Indoor Stadium.

And you start thinking about planning your fall travel.

The Malady of the Quotidian: *Perspective*

One of my favorite songs by one of my favorite singer-songwriter's is Dar Williams's "The Babysitter's Here." It's starts out, "Tonight was just great, she taught us the sign for peace." I love that it pays tribute, with wit and affection, to a mostly unsung female archetype. Ask any woman about her favorite baby-sitter and my guess is that she'll be able to come up quickly with a name, and then she'll smile. (Mine was Sherrie Morrie. She taught us the sign for peace.)

You find your role models where you can. For many girls, we start with our baby-sitters. Or we latch onto our mothers' friends: older women who are not authority figures make for good mentors. But so, too, do women teachers and, if we're lucky, those who supervise us in our jobs.

While in college I was a work-study student in Yale's French department. The secretary, Hallie, had just returned from a stint in the Peace Corps and was applying to graduate school. She was in her late twenties. She was my boss and she became my friend. It wasn't entirely a friendship of equals. She'd been out in the world and knew a lot more than I did. It was nice being with someone who was neither a college student nor a professor. I learned from her about lots of things. And I learned, too, that even when you're in your late twenties and have graduated from a good school, your life doesn't necessarily flow without ripples.

My first job after college found me working in publishing, for another strong and interesting woman. After one year, however, I was promoted, and ever since I've worked for men. It's not quite the same. I don't want to dive too deeply into the well of gender generalization, but there's a wonderful and intense—and sometimes scary—intimacy that you often find when working for and with women.

I've now aged into being on the mentor side of the equation. Guess what? It's even better. I first encountered Lauren when, as an admissions officer, I read her application to Duke University. When I met her in person I was utterly charmed by her and asked if she wanted to be my work-study student.

We spent two years working together. She'd come into the office and we'd end up talking. For hours. We talked about her classes, her family, and her struggles. I challenged her to rethink assumptions and question received wisdom. I pushed her. Hard. She'd come in the next day and say, "You know, I was thinking about what you said and . . ."—and then she'd blow me away. She really had thought about what I'd said.

Lauren has enriched my life in ways that I could never have anticipated. I feel a pride and glow in her accomplishments; I thrill to see her change and develop and mature. I learn from her. And I worry about her. A little. It's a relationship that is part mother, part sister, part older aunt, mostly friend. I guess it's kind of like being a baby-sitter. Though sometimes it seems as if she is the one doing the baby-sitting.

It's the third day of freshman year. The director has just spoken at convocation, telling the first-year students that they are the most impressive class, by "objective" standards, ever admitted to Duke: highest test scores, most valedictorians, most students who have done cool things.

I run into Benjamin, a sweet boy from Massachusetts. His face is ashen.

"What's the matter buddy," I say.

"Somebody messed up." He looks stricken.

"What?"

"Somebody made a mistake. I shouldn't have gotten in. I don't deserve to be here."

I laugh, though I suspect I shouldn't.

"You mean the person who read your application? You mean, excuse me—me? You think I made a mistake?"

"Well," now he looks both stricken and embarrassed. "Yeah."

"No," I say. "I know this. I read over twelve hundred applications last year. I didn't make a mistake. Lots of kids wrote essays about baseball. You were the only one who wrote about the connections between baseball and Taoism."

"You remember that?" He's shocked. "I can't believe you remember that."

"Hey, baby, I remember not only what you wrote, but what

others wrote about you as well. Don't worry. You deserve to be here."

But so, I thought, did a whole bunch of other kids who had not been admitted.

How much does it matter where you go to college?

Many people, especially those who went to "prestigious" colleges and universities, think that it matters. A lot. It's like a trump card you can pull out when you need it. They claim that a fancy degree can help enormously in getting that first or second job or getting into graduate or professional school. It can, in fact, help you for the rest of your life. You become part of an elite club, regardless of whether you join an actual alumni association. Each month I see in the *Yale Alumni Magazine* an advertisement for "The Right Stuff." It reads, "Date someone who knows that the Uncertainty Principle is not about first-date etiquette." It is an "introduction service" for "fellow graduates and faculty of the Ivies, Stanford, Seven Sisters, MIT, Caltech, UC Berkeley, U of Chicago, Northwestern, medical schools, and other excellent schools."

There are burgeoning retirement communities for these same people so that they can grow old together.

Does a brand-name matter? It matters because people think it matters. Folks often point out how a Harvard man will somehow work into the first five minutes of conversation the fact that he is a Harvard man. It's funny, but it's also clearly evolutionarily useful: he does it because it does something for him. You may think he's a jerk, but you will also be, on some level, impressed (unless, of course, you went to Yale). This kind of credentialing serves a purpose. It's a shorthand route to status and, like all credentials, tells you nothing in specific. You don't know if the Harvard man was admitted because he was a legacy, a football player, or the son of a rich philanthropist. You also don't how well he did in college. It's like the old joke: What do you call the person who graduates last in his medical school class? Doctor. (Feel free, by the way, to insert the fancy school of your choice here—I certainly don't mean to single out for snobbery that esteemed institution on the Charles.)

Part of what you get when attending a highly selective college or university are the benefits of a rigorous admissions process: a hand-picked class that contains more talented and accomplished people—who may also be unlike you—than any group you are ever again likely to meet. These peers often provide a better education than what you can get in a classroom. It's in conversations about string theory with fellow students in the dining halls, late night marathon sessions arguing about the existence of God, lifting weights in the gym and discussing the weirdness of the electoral college, and speaking tentatively during study breaks about the vagaries of sex, that the value of being in a select group comes out. And sure, it is also about making the friends, the connections, that will follow you through the rest of your life. Of course each of the thousands of institutions of higher education in this country has a core of students who are intellectually engaged. It's just that the selective admissions process appears to guarantee a higher percentage of peers who'd rather talk about Kant than about kegs.

However, the price of getting to be a Harvard woman, a Princetonian, an Eli, means that you may become less like yourself and more like your classmates. At most colleges there is a dominant culture. People who are eighteen to twenty-two years old are highly susceptible to acculturation. They come in as individuals— risk-taking, assumption-challenging, intellectually daring young people—and they leave as Brownies or Tigers. You notice, when you observe students during their four years of college, the "evolution" in dress, in hair styles, even in speech. Gone is the blue eyeshadow from high school, replaced by black fingernail polish. Boys from cold rural areas trade in their down parkas for cool long black overcoats from thrift stores. They look more like their classmates than they did at the beginning of their freshman year. They may also think more like their classmates: I used to say that our students entered Duke more interesting than they left it.

I was having a conversation with academic friends who teach at places with reputations for eggheady kids—Reed, Chicago, Columbia—places where I assumed that the students wouldn't be cowed by professors because "they wrote the book." What astonished me was that my friends were saying the same kinds of things about their students. The kids are more fun to teach their first year. By senior year they stop talking in class. They become intimidated not so much by their professors but by other students. They want to fit in. At Duke they may wear Abercrombie, drink beer and go to basketball games, and at the University of Chicago they tend to dress in black and smoke endless cigarettes, the resulting acculturation is not much different. They have just developed different cultural styles.

How much does it matter where you go to college? In terms of the classroom education and level of undergraduate teaching, I think there's probably not a great difference among the many "good" private schools that can afford to have small classes. I know from years in academic publishing that there are equally accomplished scholars at the big state universities. They may be, simply by the sheer fact of numbers, less accessible to their students. That does not make them any less good at teaching. There are also excellent academics stuck in the boondocks, at unfancy schools in unfancy places. The student bodies of less selective schools may enroll more kids interested in frat parties than they are in Freud. But at most schools—perhaps at all schools—there is a core of good, smart students.

Other than the size of the classes and the diversity of classmates, the curricula doesn't vary all that much, and most have placement offices and alumni networks to help in post-graduation job hunting. What you don't get at the bigger and/or less fancy schools is the cushion that makes sure you stay in school, the army of administrators who keep students in line, who help them find their way. Everyone knows the score: the more selective the college, the lower the attrition rate.

It's easy to flunk out of a big state university; it takes effort to flunk out of the Ivy League.

There are plenty of people who will tell you that they went to a perfectly stinky school and have nonetheless managed to become extremely successful, thank you very much. You don't have to look far to find them. It's also the case that some of the most interesting, most intellectually alive people I know are the autodidacts, either those who never graduated from college or, most especially, those who never went at all. They seem to have a different relationship to learning—they read because they want to, because they have not been told they have to. They are often exhausting to be with—they are so interested in talking about everything.

How much does it matter where you go to college? I think the national conversation about admissions needs to be refocused. This obsession with name-brands seems a peculiarly American phenomenon. Other countries certainly have class-bound ideas when it comes to higher education, but the multitude of private universities in this country is unparalleled, the access to further schooling remarkable. And yet, it is on a few dozen schools that a portion of the country intensely focuses its attention.

I'd like to see the discussion about admissions shift focus from "How do I get in?" to a more thoughtful and critical look at the whole system. What is the value of an elite degree? Why is the sticker that you put on the back of your car so important? Do these elite schools still deserve their reputations? How good should a "good school" be, and what does it mean to be a "good school?" What is the value added in paying elite private school tuition over that for a public school—what exactly is it that you get when you pay an order of magnitude more for schooling? Is it worth it? How important is diversity, and what do we mean by diversity? How does where you went to college shape the rest of your life? Does it?

This conversation is going on at an academic, intellectual level. There have been a spate of recent books—Robert Reich's *Future of Success*; William C. Bowen and Derek Bok's *Shape of the River: Long-Term Consequences of Considering Race in College and University Admissions*, and the more recent book by Bowen and James L. Shulman,

The Game of Life: College Sports and Educational Values; Nicholas Lehmann's *Big Test: The Secret History of the American Meritocracy*, to name just a few—that are examining these issues with tons of data and trenchant analysis. But they are not, I think, being read by the parents of college applicants. Not one parent ever demonstrated to me any larger social awareness of the process in which they were engaged, though they'd often ask what I thought of various books in the self-help category on admissions.

I would hope that parents begin to look at themselves and ask what is going on with their generation—the boomers who are raising these hypercompetitive children, who are seeing their own competitiveness played out in their kids' college admissions process. What has changed in parenting? And in high schools? Their children feel that they have to do "everything" in order to get into the "right" school. What does it mean that the *New York Times* ran a front page article about sixth graders' anxiety about their college applications, or that Kaplan has started a standardized test prep course for third graders? Shouldn't the parents be protecting their kids from this kind of insanity rather than encouraging it? Make no mistake, the admissions industry is clearly fostering this. The national admissions organization has begun inviting middle school kids to its college fairs.

The baby boomer parents who grew up in a recession want their kids to have every break possible. If a brand-name degree is going to help them get that first job, then that's what they want. The kids themselves don't know what they want. At age seventeen, their priorities are weird and random. They believe that one visit will tell them what a school is really like. They are also, for some reason obscure to me, encouraged to know what they want to do once they get to college. There's a meaninglessness in the clarity with which some of these kids plan out their careers: "I want to be a lawyer"; "I want to go into business." They have no idea, usually, what it's like to work in these fields. What if they come to college and decide they love classical philology, or the study of the Tibetan diaspora, or the history of Shaker furniture? What if they come to college and are never exposed to disciplines they've never heard of, sticking instead to some ill-conceived childhood ambition?

Going to college is about making a separation from home. It should be about going toward rather than a running from. There's a lot to be said, I think, for taking a year off between high school and college. I would recommend that students do it only after being admitted and then deferring their enrollment; it's hard to go through the application process once you've left high school. Many of the kids I know could have used a break before they started college. One of my favorite kids, one of the best applicants I ever read, was at the top of his high school class, had great board scores, and incredible teacher recommendations; he wrote a poignant and insightful essay and he did everything in his school, including serving on the hiring committee for a new principal. A clear auto admit. He got to Duke and was overwhelmed by the freedom to not do anything. He stopped going to class. He dropped out just before the end of his first semester. He just wasn't ready to be back in school, he said. So he bummed around, visiting friends at other colleges, living on the beach, not doing much of anything. By the next fall, he was back at Duke, more mature, more focused, and much more happy.

My experience as an admissions officer at Duke showed me the arbitrariness of the process, from all sides: From the way that kids decided on their "perfect school," the way parents pushed them in their applications, and most especially, the way decisions about applicants were made. The process is brutal, stressful, not always meritocratic, and rarely fair. But overall, it is just human, all too human. *Ecce homo.*

Most admissions officers would make similar decisions on the auto admits and the auto denies, at least that's the theory. Of course reader ratings varied widely, but for the kids at both the top and the bottom—a small fraction of the entire pool—there was a certain consistency in the decisions. It was the huge mass in the middle—the "middle muddle" one of the associates used to call it—where they were all good kids, had all done well in high school, and had similar board scores as well as similar honors, awards, and extracurricular activities, where the pride and prejudices of individual readers came into play.

The kids with the most access to information, generally those from upper-middle-class families, are going to be advantaged while applying. There are ways to play the game, and they will find out the helpful gambits. The most important thing they need to know is to be themselves. At the same time, they must recognize the things that are not unique to them. The service that independent college counselors can provide, it seems to me, is in telling kids when they sound like everyone else. Yes, you work hard.

Everyone works hard. Yes, you're a perfectionist. Everyone applying to these schools is a perfectionist. Now what is it about you that is different? They don't know, and won't know until someone tells them what the stock replies are and asks them to think more deeply about themselves. It could actually be a revealing and interesting and useful process, trying to figure out who you are so that you can present yourself to an admissions committee. It rarely is.

The more important service that counseling provides is in coming up with a good list of schools. There are so many great schools to choose from, some with less recognizable names, that most kids are completely lost at the beginning of the process. They don't know where to start, so they start with the rankings. Not a good beginning. There's plenty of detailed information available on each college and university—books and Web sites in addition to the school's own marketing materials—but nothing can replace being able to talk to someone about your interests and desires and getting suggestions of schools that might be a good fit.

There was almost no tracking, at Duke, between admissions and academic achievement on the college level. While in selection committee, and especially during alum and development rounds, I often thought to myself (and occasionally said aloud) that I supposed that someone had to be at the bottom of Duke's graduating class. I'd rather it be the rich kids and the athletes than those from underrepresented minority groups or lower-income families. But that, of course, is not the way the world works. In my unscientific, anecdotal experience, the rich kids did fine, academically and especially socially. The athletes were taken care of, both by the athletic department and by their teammates. Often, it seemed, it was the African American kids who struggled. Not so much with their schoolwork, but with trying to feel at home. Many of the African American students choose to live in Duke-owned apartments on the edge of the campus. White students think this is because they want to keep to themselves, that they "self-segregate." What I hear from my African American friends is that they prefer to clean their own bathrooms rather than to live in the squalor that children of privilege leave behind them, waiting for some invisible person to clean up their mess. Plus, the on-campus apartments are cheaper.

I was talking once to one of the men's basketball players. We'd just walked past a poster, one of the annual posters done by the athletic department featuring the team. In this one they were dressed in white linens, sipping cool drinks on a cool lawn in front of a white columned mansion. The caption read simply, "Tradition." We'd been talking about race at Duke, and this player, readily identified as African American, said the issue never came up for him. I asked him what he thought about the poster. Not much he said. I asked if he knew that many of the African American employees of the university referred to Duke as "the Plantation." He didn't. He could, it seems, afford not to think about race.

Many of the African American students that I know feel as if they are doing their time at Duke. They are the quickest of all Duke students to criticize the school. But these kids are driven. They work hard. You don't see them walking around in tatty clothes. They go to class and pay attention, often sitting in the front rows. They have their eyes on the prize, and they know—and their parents know—how much a Duke degree will mean to their future employers.

So, as much as current practice of admissions is a perpetuator of class bias, the outcome can also be something of a class leveler. I think about the African American guys on Duke's football team. Sure, they stink at football and are the laughingstock of the league. But when they graduate, they will have a Duke degree. I think about the rural valedictorians, the first-generation college kids. How different their lives will be from those of their parents. They will have different kinds of choices. I think about my working-class kids who go home to their parents and see, for the first time, that they are working class. I wonder about the children of privilege. Do they realize that they did not get in on their own merits? How could they not know? It rankles me when these same kids argue in the conservative student publications against Affirmative Action and other progressive social programs.

While working as an admissions officer I felt that I was in it, but not of it. Looking back, I see that I was more of it than I wanted to believe. It's hard not to get caught up in the chase, hard not to try to make your school sound better and more appealing than others, hard not to take it personally when the kids you most like turn "you" down for other schools. I got carried away by my own competitiveness. I wanted to win. I wanted to do a good job. I wanted big numbers of applicants from my region. I kept track of the "Why Duke?" essays that answered, "Rachel." I wanted to have the best kids to talk about during reading and selection committee. I wanted them all to come to Duke, to come to me. I became, in spite of myself, a believer in the process at the same time that I thought I saw all of the obvious flaws.

But I did see some things. I realized that there was a population of smart kids who were being disadvantaged by the way we—the way I—did recruiting. Feeling guilty, I decided to spend a few of my recruiting days my last year at city schools in Boston and San Francisco where the kids did not apply to Duke. I went because I felt that they were not getting good advice about the college application process. When I heard the kinds of questions kids were asking, I saw that they were getting no advice at all. I talked not about Duke in particular, but about the way the system works. I talked about the availability of federal financial need-based aid and merit scholarships. I talked about Affirmative Action. I was the only admissions officer they'd ever met. Pro bono work is often the most satisfying.

I would like to see college admissions become deprofessionalized. Many schools involve their faculty in admissions decisions. This seems right to me. Not only because they have to teach these students, but because unless admissions suddenly and inexplicably becomes more attractive to intellectuals, faculty are going to be better at reading and selection. Now, it is true that professorial involvement can produce problems. Duke's School of Engineering has for many years used faculty members to serve on selection committee. Walking into a room full of white men, aged fifty to death, who didn't believe in diversity and did believe in standardized testing, was, for me, an exercise in frustration. My last year in admissions saw the hiring of a new dean of engineering, a woman who seems committed to progressive understandings of the world. I hope that she will be able to effect a change. It will not be easy.

Apart from who reads the applications, I think that the format should also change. Currently, the process is designed to encourage as many applications as possible. That's a mandate not just from the deans and directors of admissions but from the presidents and trustees of universities. If you really want to select a class that is appropriate for your institution, it makes more sense to have less common applications. It means having to define more specifically the kinds of students you want and what kind of an institution you are and want to be—just looking for "the best" applicants will not suffice. The University of Chicago seems to recognize this. Their application is incredibly, ridiculously specific to them. The only kids who apply to Chicago are kids who want to go there—otherwise it's just not worth the effort.

I would like to see admissions offices require graded high school papers—a truer indication of academic ability—both of the student and her teachers—than essays polished by highly paid professionals. Or have colleges follow the medical school model, with a general application that can generate a secondary application, if the school wants to pursue the applicant, perhaps requiring an essay with a quick turnaround time, asking a question specific to the school, by hand, if you want to keep the fingers of professionals off them. Or if students are willing to make the trip to visit a school and interview, give them a quiz, an essay test, on the spot. Ask them to solve a logic problem if they say they want to be engineer. See how they think when there's no one else around to help them think.

At the very least, I'd like to see more schools giving more weight to the teacher recommendations. These are the one part of the process that cannot be manipulated or controlled. Students rarely focus on this part of the application and parents almost never do. It's hard to write a good recommendation. Anyone who's ever been asked knows how time-consuming it is to do justice to the person you are talking about. It's also hard to read so many of them, especially when they have been written by weary, over-worked teachers. But this, it seems to me, is a key to doing college admissions well.

It would help to have larger admissions staffs—or smaller applicant pools. It would also help to make an effort to recruit more intellectually astute people to read these applications. Schools are spending more and more money on recruitment: more weeks of travel, glossier marketing materials, bigger direct-mail campaigns. The *Yale Alumni Magazine* announced that its office of admissions has hired its first "director of recruitment," someone not encumbered by having to read applications who can spend time thinking only about how to get the numbers up. Duke is similarly boosting its budget for recruitment both of applications and of admitted, but not yet matriculated, students (you not only need big application numbers, you need a high "yield" percentage of the students you accept to look good in the rankings). Do these places really believe that there are thousands more good students out there who just aren't applying? And do they really think that having merely enthusiastic staff will help them to recruit not just more but better students?

Change would be welcome; it seems at this point unlikely. The stakes, for reasons having to do mostly with issues around social class, are high. Parents are desperate. Kids are busy. Alumni are drunk with nostalgia. Prep schools have been caught lying both about their applicants and on their reports of college acceptances. Admissions officers are often not as smart as the applicants they are denying. While admission to a first-choice school may not be impossible, the odds are against most kids.

I was far from an ideal admissions officer. I was so adept at managing to avoid on-call duty that on those occasions when I was forced to answer the random questions that came in during the course of a normal day I was at a loss. Do we actually require three years of foreign language? I'd have to ask a colleague. In a detail-oriented world, I was a person who saw the forest and couldn't recognize a tree if I skied into it. I was not intimidated by the faculty and argued, against the grain, to have them more involved in the admissions process. I had a smidgen of disdain for some of my colleagues—and my superiors—and was frequently heard by those closest to me muttering under my breath, "Just not smart enough . . ." Nor did I have that warm and welcoming professionally dressed flight attendant quality that many of my coworkers displayed, making everyone feel comfortable and at home. I got impatient, answered questions I considered obnoxious in obnoxious ways. I pointed out to the mothers who said, "We're juniors," that no, "we" were not in fact juniors.

I did like the kids, I liked the travel, and I liked staying at home to read. But as much as I enjoyed parts of my job, I'm glad to be out of the business. I have no interest in giving advice to anyone about what they should do in order to be admitted to Duke or to any other school. As I've tried to show in this book, there are many variables that are beyond the control of applicants—and sometimes of admissions officers. You may be able to spiff up your application, but no one can guarantee results. Anyone who tells you differently is either naive or wants your money. The bottom line is that it's still a game, a game of mostly chance and some skill. If someone else had been reading my region, no doubt different decisions would have been made. Would they have been better decisions? Maybe from the point of view of a handful of students, but overall, no. Just different.

There are many wonderful colleges and universities, small and large, private and public, in this country. There is federal financial aid—and numerous outside scholarships—available so that, theoretically at least, everyone should be able to afford an education. The notion of a perfect school or a perfect degree is as ridiculous as it is pernicious. Students should take time in high school to pursue actual interests rather than résumé-padding activities. They should also realize that unless they discover a protein or publish a novel, they are going to look a lot like all of the other qualified applicants. If they don't get in to their first-choice school, they need to know that they are not being found lacking as a person; it is their application that is being denied.

Besides, after a couple of weeks it's likely that whatever college they end up going to—even if it's their safety school—will become their first choice.

After three years of working in Duke's Office of Undergraduate Admissions I knew I was finished. I'd learned a lot but wanted to move on. I decided, in the late spring of my last year, that I would quit, and instead of finding another job, I would try to write a book about admissions.

When I announced this intention to Audrey she expressed no surprise. I was surprised that she was not surprised. This seemed a novel and interesting idea to me—I was surprised by it. Why wasn't she?

"For the entire first year that you worked here," she told me, "Missy was convinced that you were planted as a spy."

"What? You're kidding, right?"

"No, I am not kidding. She was convinced that they had sent you to work here and then write about the office."

"Who are *they*?"

"She didn't know."

"How did you respond to this?"

"So what? That's what I said to her. So what if she writes about us? If you don't do anything you're ashamed of, why should it matter?"

Admissions is an art, not a science. That's what admissions people like to say.

Acknowledgments

When I quit admissions—the third time I'd left a job without having another lined up—people thought, again, that I was either brave or crazy. Perhaps I am a little of both, or perhaps neither. The simple truth is that I am fortunate to be well loved. I have in my life a core group of people who give me the confidence to do scary things, who support me emotionally, and who make sure that I get enough to eat.

I could not have written this book without my family, which is warm, extended, and a little odd. It includes my mother, always a source of inspiration, amusement, and occasional and expected motherly vexation; her partner, my honorary father, George Rhoads, the most wonderful nut I know; my overly generous brother, Mark Toor; and Mark's sanguine wife, Allyn Turner. I also include in my family the REBs, the fraternal brotherhood of Rachel's Ex-Boyfriends: Andrew Krystal and Michael Bergmann. Mike is perhaps the most dependable and practical person I have ever met and has been a stabilizing—and loving—influence ever since he entered my life as my physics tutor. Andrew is the person I can tell it to. And with the aid of a small amount of caffeine, his cleverness is sometimes as helpful as it is diverting. Valerie Chang insists on tying me to the Real World and makes me talk about things I hate—taxes, in particular. I know she is only trying to help. She worries about me. Hannah, whom it seems reductive to describe as a dog, also worries about me. She's a worrying kind of dog. But she has also given me years of delight, pleasure, and love. Just after I left admissions, Emma the pig became ill and passed away. When I think about reading applications, the process is bound up with the breaks I took to cuddle with my girls, Hannah and Emma, or to take walks. Emma liked to go for walks. There was always a good chance of finding something to eat. I miss the little pig. My mother, George, Mark and Allyn, Mike and Andrew, Val, and, of course, Hannah: they are my family. I am linguistically inadequate to fully express my love for them.

Much of this book was written while I house-sat in Aptos, California, for my friends Michele and Steve Shaw. My Berkeley relatives, Gary Lapow, Ahbi Vernon, and Zev and Emerald Vernon-Lapow, helped me through the crisis of Emma's death as well as just being fun to hang out with. My Ride-and-Tie partner, Mary Tiscornia, offered fun outings—she ran with me, raced with me, and taught me to jump on her gigantic thoroughbred, Wilbur. I loved being in California and am grateful to my friends on the left coast.

You never know what little thing is going to change the course of your life. An unexpected E-mail from Karen Winkler at *The Chronicle of Higher Education* launched me into wanting to write essays and gave me the opportunity to do so. I never knew, when I was in publishing, what it was like to be on the receiving end of good editing. Let me tell you, it's great. Carl Elliott started out as an author, became a friend—through four or five years of almost daily E-mail—and edited me into becoming a writer. He is my touchstone. Chad

Massie, former colleague, admissions maven, and good friend, read through the manuscript line by line and, as is he wont, helped to gentle me and remind me of what I'd forgotten or overlooked. After a hiatus of ten years I was lucky to run into Dave Mankin again. He turned his philological eye to my writing, correcting my grammar and helping me think through a lot of issues relating to admissions. He also provided a goodly amount of care and feeding. Former author, Rod Smolla, offered legal advice and much-appreciated praise. Peter Klopfer has not only read everything I've written and given insightful suggestions but has coached my running, let me ride his horses, and provided intellectual companionship. While often more voluble with criticism than with praise, he is in fact one of the most generous people I have ever met. Peter and Martha Klopfer have welcomed me—as they have many others—into their family, and I am grateful.

My Duke kids provide spark in my life. I hesitate to mention them by name for fear of the many I will no doubt inadvertently leave out: My "Rachelettes" know who they are. I must acknowledge, though, the special relationship I have with Lauren Vose, my "Mini-Me," who started out as an applicant, worked for me for two years, and is now a woman I am proud to call friend. During our Friday breakfasts Lauren provided me with intellectual stim, a whole lot of laughs, and loving warmth.

I am most grateful to the following people, Duke student friends, for the use, in this book, of the essays that helped to get them into Duke and made me want to know them: Tim Van Voris, Marisa Gonzalez, Erin Sager, Eric Weinberger, Jennifer Koontz,

Edward Nam, and Margaret Harris. I'd also like to thank the two students who let me use their essays but asked that their names not be published.

Much of what I do and think is influenced by my friendship with Julius Scott, who, as I tell him often, and now can say in print, is the smartest person I know.

I received help and guidance from friends and colleagues in admissions. No doubt this is not a book that any of them would have written. Some admissions officers worried that the publication of this book would make their jobs harder. I hope that is not the case.

While in publishing, I always believed that literary agents were scum. Robin Rue changed all that. She not only guided me through the process of trade publishing, but she insisted that it be fun. She fluffed me when I needed fluffing and told me to go take a long run when that was what I needed. Elizabeth Beier has been enthusiastic about this book from the beginning and proved a graceful and energetic editor. Robin and Elizabeth understood where I wanted to go with this book, and they helped me get there. All mistakes, infelicities of language, and wrongheaded opinions, are, of course, mine.